D0888838

T-34
Russian Armor

Douglas Orgill

BB

Editor-in-Chief: Barrie Pitt
Editor: David Mason
Art Director: Sarah Kingham
Picture Editor: Robert Hunt
Designer: David Allen
Cover: Denis Piper
Special Drawings: John Batchelor
Photographic Research: Nan Shuttleworth
Cartographer: Richard Natkiel

Contents

Juggernaut

Introduction by Kenneth Macksey

This book, written with such verve by Douglas Orgill, a man with personal experience of tank warfare, is the story of a juggernaut – the tale of the T34 tank which was the dominant weapon in the hands of the Russian tank force in the Second World War. Therefore when one remembers that the core of a Russian assault at any period was almost always the tank element – heftily supported by artillery and air power – it becomes clear that Orgill is describing the kernel of the campaigns on the Eastern Front between 1941 and 1945.

Only occasionally throughout the history of war have single new weapon systems appeared which have, in the flash of a battle, redoubled tempo, radically changed values and made an indelible mark on the future of combat. A weapon such as this was the original tank when first it came into action in 1916, its importance to be found not so much in its immediate impact on the battle nor even upon the minds of soldiers, but essentially with a gradual realisation that the first shock of technical surprise was as nothing to the enduring qualities inherent in its structure. Here was a weapon which could be developed both in technical form and in its employment. Here was the instigation of an international race for the lead in both tank technology and techniques – a race which had turned several corners before a T34 fired its first shot in anger in 1941. Nevertheless the first T34s which blundered into action that summer – strong in armour, rich in power plant and of deadly lethality – were almost invariably wasted by commanders and crews who had neither the wit nor the training to make use of this, the best tank then in service in the world. And the fact that two years later the same basic machine was holding its own against a new breed of superior German tanks is by

no means an indication that Russian training standards and the original excellence of the tank had been improved all that much. The fact was that by 1943, the Russians could manufacture at least five tanks to every new German machine – and the ease with which T34 could be churned out in mass and manned by crewmen of the most dubious mechanical aptitude was the real tribute to Russian industry and the men who had designed the T34 in the first place.

I well remember a colleague describing a journey through Poland just after the war and recalling the sight of Russian tank carcasses still rusting in clutches before the torn remains of isolated German tanks. Mark IVs, Panthers and Tigers frequently massacred T34s, KVs and JSs at small relative loss to themselves. Yet no matter how many Russian tanks each German crew sent up in flames, the same fate was eventually assured for

them for when, even if they temporarily survived, there was even less chance of receiving a battle worthy replacement in which to carry on the work of destruction.

If the ultimate test of a basic tank design is its adaptability and durability, T34 and its variants have long ago passed that test. To this day the lesser Russian satellite nations make good use of the original T34s and the shape of even the latest T62 is strikingly similar to that of its great forbear. Meanwhile the Russian Army remains irrevocably committed to the employment of massed tanks in any war they might fight during the next decade or so. Suffer whatever casualties modern anti-tank weapons might inflict upon them, the Russians believe they can afford to gain their objectives with a flood of T34s successors manned, we may assume, by crews who understand their duties better than did their fathers in 1941.

Birth of
a weapon

Of all the weapons met by the German army during the Second World War, none came as more of a shock to the German soldier than the Russian T-34 tank in the summer of 1941. The dazzling success of the panzer campaign in France in the previous year had reinforced the carefully-nurtured Nazi belief in German superiority. Now the revelation that the *Untermenschen* – the subhumans, as Nazi philosophy dismissed the Russians – could have evolved a weapon which seemed to be considerably in advance of its German counterparts, came as a fright to Hitler's soldiers, high and low. One by one, the German panzer leaders paid it sombre tribute.

'Very high quality,' said Major-General F W von Mellenthin, Chief of Staff of XLVIII Panzer Corps. 'We had nothing comparable . . .' For Field-Marshal Ewald von Kleist, of First Panzer Army, it was 'the finest tank in the world . . .'The gloomiest estimate, from the German point of view, was made by the greatest tank soldier of them all, Colonel-General Heinz Guderian, commanding Second Panzer Army: 'Very worrying . . . up to this time we had enjoyed tank superiority, but from now on the situation was reversed. The prospect of rapid, decisive victories was fading in consequence . . .'

Yet, as will be seen, the T-34 had many defects as a fighting machine. It was a typical product of the society which produced it, concentrating solely on a list of absolute essentials, spurning any kind of sophistication and even the kind of internal comfort considered, farther west, to be necessary for effective operation by its crew. Nevertheless, it succeeded, in its day, in solving the basic equation which should be written in gold above every tank designer's desk: the effectiveness of a weapon is directly equal to its ability to get itself properly into position to deal decisive blows without being harmed by the blows it

A column of T-34s on the move

Above left: T-34s in the infantry support role: spring 1942. *Left:* Vulnerable Russian soldiers ride to battle on the back of the T-34: Stalingrad area, autumn 1942. *Above:* BT-2 Tank

is itself receiving. This proposition is almost child-like in its simplicity, but Russian tank designers had understood it more completely than those in charge of British or German tank production in the years before 1941. That was the sole reason why the T-34 appeared to be a wonder-weapon when the panzer divisions first met it in the summer dust of the Russian steppe.

The genesis of the T-34 lay far back from 1941, in the years which followed the German defeat in the First World War. Ironically, it was the Germans themselves who gave the Russians their first clear ideas about tanks. In the early 1920s, Lenin, concerned about the rebuffs suffered by the Red Army in the short war with Poland, in the course of which the Poles had actually captured Kiev, turned for help and advice to the other outcast of Europe, defeated Germany. General Hans von Seeckt, in charge of the reorganisation of the German army, was himself looking for ways of circumventing the restrictive military clauses of the Treaty of Versailles, which had abolished the general staff, and had forbidden Germany to possess tanks, military aircraft, or weapons of offence.

German and Russian officers met. The result was the policy which the Germans called *Abmachungen* – German-Russian co-operation and collaboration, under which a joint training centre for tank warfare was secretly set up in the depths of Russia. This was at Kazan, a city on the Volga which was surrounded by open countryside giving excellent facilities for tank training. Both Russian and German tank models were tried out at Kazan – the German prototypes having to be shipped there in pieces because of the need for secrecy. The training programme was drawn up in Berlin and the instructors were German. They noted that the Russian officers, some of whom had been NCOs in the former Tsarist army, were 'industrious students who applied almost to the letter any instruction received. They took down every word and learned it by heart . . .'

Meanwhile, the Soviet Government bought tanks from abroad. In 1930,

Colonel-General Heinz Guderian

Field-Marshal Ewald von Kleist

sixty British machines were purchased – 12-ton, 6-ton, and light Carden Loyd models. Two years later they were followed by two examples of the new 10-ton fast tank which was then being demonstrated by the American tank designer J Walter Christie. This machine had a new kind of suspension which gave it in a later version 64.3mph on wheels, and nearly 40mph on tracks. To this tank the T-34, though it was not yet dreamed of, can trace its direct descent.

These various tanks, assembled hotch-potch from the bourgeois West, became the basis on which Soviet tank designers built the Russian armoured force of the next decade. It was an immense force. The great explosion of talent and energy which now took place in the field of Russian tank production is one of the most remarkable developments in the history of armaments. In 1924 the first lorry was built inside the boundaries of the Soviet state; by 1939 Russia had assembled tank forces which in number greatly exceeded the combined total of the rest of the armies of the world. The equipment of these forces varied in quality, but some of the Russian machines, in their day, were as good as or better than anything in general service elsewhere.

Much, at first, was copied from British designs, especially after the Russo-German tank school at Kazan was wound up when Hitler came to power. The Carden Loyd machine became the basis for the light, turretless Russian T-27; the Vickers 6-tonner of the T-26. Other models were more purely Russian in inspiration – a 29-ton T-28 and a 45-ton T-35, both of them multi-turreted designs intended for independent operations. Neither tank was a success, but each carried an indication that Russian armoured theory was at least clear in definition: that a tank was a moving platform for a weapon, and that if the weapon was inadequate, the tank was doomed. The T-28 had a 76.2mm gun, while the T-35

Above: T-34/76 C, armed with 76.2mm gun of 41.2 calibres. *Below:* Vickers 6-ton tank, the type purchased by the Soviet government in 1930

Above: The pull of the wide track: BT7s tackle practice anti-tank ditches on manoeuvres: July 1941. *Below:* An American ancestor: the T-3 medium suspension Christie

carried a 76.2mm and two 45mm guns. Undergunning was one error which could not be laid at the door of Russian designers, whereas, by contrast, British medium tanks of the period were still armed with the three-pounder (equivalent to 47mm), soon to be superseded by the even smaller two-pounder (40mm).

A new path was opened for Russian tank design when the two Christie models were purchased. These tanks were the final product of many years of thought and experiment by Christie, an American automotive engineer who had entered the field of mechanised war in 1916 with an anti-aircraft gun carriage, and had developed his ideas through tanks of varying success until they reached full fruition in the revolutionary M-1931 (later called the T-3 in the United States Army). Christie himself summed up the thinking behind this

machine when he wrote: 'It is an established fact, conceded by everyone who reads and thinks, that manpower in defence of a country is fast fading away, and that machines swift and low as a trench line are being substituted for manpower.

'My first object was to build a chassis that will protect the man who is to risk his life by facing the enemy, and to provide a machine by the use of which he can defend himself and destroy the enemy. Therefore we built a chassis with frontal lines and slopes that will make it almost impossible to penetrate the chassis with any type of projectile. Next we constructed the chassis as low as possible, making it as inconspicuous as the power plant permits. We then turned to the next problem of defense, which is speed. With speed you can surround the enemy, you can flank him, you can reach points quickly and take up positions to stop the advance. If you meet an overpowering force you can quickly evade it . . .'

Christie's definition of a tank was perfect, but, ironically, his ideas on the future of war were less realistic in terms of the conflict in Europe which was already on the horizon. They belonged to the more extravagant theories of armoured warfare which were in vogue in a small British coterie of the time, led by Generals Fuller and Hobart, but supported only part of the way – and with significant reservations – by Liddell Hart. These theories, implicitly, saw the battlefield of the future as resembling the sea rather than the land. Listen to Hobart, talking in 1934:

'The tank brigade must move rapidly and be able to appear and disappear. It must avoid unnecessary losses. It must be very flexible and controllable and continually manoeuvre so as to threaten a number of objectives. It must induce enemy concentrations in one direction and then move suddenly sixty or seventy miles elsewhere. It must be able to strike rapidly, carrying out effective

15

Above: Soviet T-26/C in winter action, 1942. *Below:* Soviet T-26s in winter camouflage

destruction in two or three hours and withdraw rapidly and leave the enemy uncertain of its whereabouts. It must be able to disperse into small columns in order to mislead the enemy, and to reunite as required; it must be capable of completely controlled movement by day and night . . .'

These were tactics made for Christie's dream, but their naval character is unmistakeable. They would have received the hearty approval of John Paul Jones, or, before him, of Sir Francis Drake. Except for the deceptive moment of panzer glory in France in 1940, they bore little relation to the true nature of the war that was to be fought in Western and Southern Europe between 1939 and 1945. Yet they were significantly nearer in spirit to the kind of war that might be fought in the vast Russian spaces, and it was from these tactics that Soviet Russia – perhaps because she was concerned only with her own geographical problems – evolved a tank, the T-34, which was peculiarly suited to reign as queen of such a battlefield. This was because Russian designers adopted both the dream and the machine to make them fit the realities of a campaign in Russia.

They began with Christie's tank. Christie was at heart an automotive engineer rather than a builder of weapons, and the T-3 reflected this limitation. He was preoccupied with speed, sometimes to an absurd degree, as when he tried to produce vehicles which could evade air attack. The T-3, with its three-man crew – driver, gunner, and commander – repeated the light tank heresy which was then the cult of the British army by being armed with a 37mm gun. The significance of his machine lay in its suspension – an ingenious arrangement of springs and large road wheels that permitted a considerable vertical wheel displacement when moving at speed over rough ground, though it produced an undulating gun platform which inhibited firing on the move. It was, however, the world's first truly fast tank.

Russian officers, less rooted in military conservatism than their opposite numbers in the West, were swift to see the T-3's potentialities for the sheer geographical task of any armoured force operating in Russia. The two models which were purchased were tested at Voronezh in 1931, and arrangements were immediately made to produce a Russian copy. This was built at the tank factory at Kharkov, and was known simply as the *bystro-khodnii tank* – literally, the fast-moving tank. The designation was shortened to BT, and the BT-1 became the first of a celebrated series which was to culminate, after considerable changes, in the T-34.

It was followed between 1931 and 1938 by the BT-2, BT-3, BT-5, BT-7, and BT-8. The feature common to all these models was the Christie suspension, the ability to move from tracks to wheels and back again to tracks, and sloped armour designed to minimise the impact of anti-tank projectiles. More significantly, the series was progressively up-gunned, from the 37mm gun of the BT-1, through the 45mm of the BT-3, to an eventual 76.2mm on the BT-8.

This was possible because the Russians were not putting all their eggs into one basket. Heavier tank guns were easily available for the BT series because they were also producing heavier tanks. The BT models were coming off the production lines in considerable numbers: indeed, by 1935 there were about 3,500, of all marks, in service. But Russian designers were now launching out on the production of bigger, more traditional models like the T-28 and the T-35 already mentioned. The gun of the T-28 was a 76.2mm, 16.5 calibres long; soon it was replaced by a more powerful model 26 calibres long. Such a steady advance in the length and power of tank armament was in sharp contrast with practice in Britain, where even the heaviest tank, the Matilda, mounted only the two-

Above: German Mark IV with short 7.5cm gun. *Below:* BT-7s on parade in Moscow, May Day 1940

pounder. In Germany, the Mark IV, of which only a few were in service for the Battle of France, mounted a 75mm gun, but it was a short low-velocity version which was feeble in an armour-piercing role. In addition, like the Mark IV – but unlike the Matilda – the Soviet tanks were fitted with turrets which were capable of taking guns which were larger than the original specification – a considerable production advantage as the gun-armour race slowly began to gather pace.

More important still from the point of view of the future development of the Russian armoured force, the production of the BT series was accompanied, in a mood of growing technical confidence, by one of the most efficient design teams in the history of armaments. This group was headed by Mikhail Ilyich Koshkin, a graduate of a Leningrad institute of technology, who had worked on an earlier experimental wheel-and-track design known as the T-29. Koshkin now designed the last tank to derive its characteristics entirely from the BT series. This was the wheel-and-track A-20 of 1937–38. It was a direct forerunner of the T-34 – an 18-ton, fast-medium machine, with sloped armour that was 25mm thick on the turret, and a 45mm gun. Because of its now-familiar built-in option of wheel or track locomotion, it was steered by a steering wheel. The A-20 was considered to be too light for its role, and it was followed in 1939 by the T-32, a heavier cruiser tank moving on tracks alone. This latter feature was due to the urging of Koshkin. Superficially, the wheel-or-track option may have seemed a desirable one: a tank on wheels causes greatly less damage to the road system over which it moves, and it can also travel at much greater speed. However, the realities of campaigning conditions made the option virtually meaningless – and it would be an added complication in the simple, uncluttered tank production line which Koshkin was aiming at. He wanted a medium tank with a better gun, a tank that was simple to produce, and which could be handled by very varied manufacturing facilities ranging from the technically sophisticated to the comparatively simple. In his preliminary report on the T-32, he put forward the view that because 'of the tactical reluctance to employ the BT tanks in the wheeled role, added to the technical difficulties associated with producing a tank which is able to travel on both wheels and tracks . . . it is suggested that future efforts should be directed towards the development of a less complex vehicle, running on tracks alone . . .'

With his colleagues Alexander Morozov and Nikolai Kucherenko, he now began to design the T-34. He was already a sick man: within two years he would be dead of a chest disease. But his was the brain which drew so many of the correct conclusions from earlier experience with the BT models, and which now moulded those conclusions into the design of a weapon which, though not faultless, almost alone among tanks met the needs of its time.

Initial work on the new tank was swift. The design work was completed at the end of 1939, and two prototypes quickly followed. Early in 1940 these two machines were sent on the gruelling course which the Russian tank production bureau imposed – a 2,000 mile test run, in the heart of winter, from their birthplace at Kharkov to Moscow, and back home through Smolensk and Kiev.

Thus the T-34 was born. It was the production not of inspirational genius but of robust common-sense. It owed its existence to men who could envisage a mid-century battlefield more clearly than anyone in the West, except for a handful of theorists, had been able to do. The work which the Koshkin design team carried out at the Kharkov locomotive works in 1939 was to change the history of the war, and thus of Europe and the world.

The first T-34

The new tank had a battle-weight, fully equipped, of 27 tons 16 hundred-weight. Its overall length was 21 feet 7 inches, measured to the front of the somewhat overhanging 76.2mm gun. It was eight feet high, with a track width of 19 inches, and a ground clearance of 16 inches. It had a crew of four – a driver and a hull gunner in the front of the tank, and a turret crew of two. These were a loader, and a commander who also doubled as gunner. Tanks in 1940 were a good deal less sophisticated, particularly from the point of view of crew comfort, than they have since become – and this Russian tank was in this respect worse than most. An examination of the equipment and duties of the four Russians in the T-34 shows that they did not have an easy task.

The driver sat at the left-front of the tank, in a cushioned armchair-type seat with a folding back-rest which was not adjustable in any way. He controlled a 500-horse-power, partly aluminium diesel engine, the V-2. This was a remarkably economic 12-cylinder unit, with a capacity of 38.9 litres, producing its 500 horse-power at 1,800 revolutions per minute. This engine had been designed in 1935 by two Russian engineers, J Vickman and T Czupachin, but it also may well have owed a great deal to a Fiat aero engine of the same period, to which it bears a strong resemblance.

The driver's controls were conventional for a tank. The steering wheel which had been a feature of earlier BT models and of the A-20 was gone, and steering was by means of orthodox steering levers which controlled track speeds. For the rest, the driver had the usual clutch, footbrake and accelerator, mounted from left to right respectively, as in a motor car. His instruments were the bare minimum necessary for efficient operation. On a panel in front of his eyes were the dials

T-34s and infantry assemble for Timoshenko attack on the South-western Front, April 1942

of the water temperature gauge,
calibrated from 0-125 degrees Centi-
grade; the oil temperature gauge
similarly marked; and the oil pressure
gauge from 0-15 kilogrammes per
square centimetre. On a further panel
to the driver's left were the remainder
of the instruments: a rev counter from
400-3,000; a speedometer; an ammeter
from 0-50 amps; a voltmeter 0-50 volts,
and the starter switch. Starting was
electrical but a compressed air system
was fitted for use in emergency.
Finally, the gearbox had three forward and one reverse gear, though in
later models this was improved to a
five-gear box, of the sliding mesh type.

The hull-gunner sat on the driver's
right, in an identical seat. His gun was
a 7.62mm Degtyarev gas-operated
machine-gun, which had been developed for tank use from an infantry
weapon of the previous decade. It was
fed by a 60-shot drum-type magazine,
and its maximum rate of fire was
500–600 rounds a minute – though a
more realistic and less wasteful figure
in action might be around one-
hundred rounds a minute.

The turret itself was cramped, even
for only two men, and it is clear that
this must have impaired the commander's performance. In addition to

commanding the tank, he had also to
lay and fire the gun, and the turret
gave him only fifty-six inches of head
room in which to work. Both commander and loader sat on padded seats
which were adjustably mounted on a
tubular support, each provided with a
wide cushioned backrest fitted to the
turret ring. Since the crew's seats were
themselves attached to the turret
ring, they did not revolve with the
gun as the turret was traversed – unlike many Western tanks in which the
whole turret basket, with its rotating
floor, moved with the gun. The turret
crew of the T-34 could follow the
traverse only by squirming in their
seats as the gun swung round.

The commander controlled two
guns – the 76.2mm main armament,
and a 7.62mm Degtyarev machine-gun
mounted coaxially beside it. The
76.2mm gun was an excellent dual-
purpose weapon, firing either high-
explosive or armour-piercing rounds.
The early versions of the T-34 mounted
a 76.2mm gun which was 30.5 calibres

long, but this was soon superseded by an improved model 41.2 calibres long. This weapon was capable of penetrating 69mm of armour at 500 yards or 54mm at about a mile – more than enough, as we shall see, to deal with the principal German tanks which opposed it in 1941.

The turret guns were sighted either by means of a periscope dial sight, or by a cranked telescopic sight mounted at the side of the gun. The periscope sight had a moveable top prism, and illuminated moving graticules. The man at the gun could deflect the crosswires of the sights on to the target by adjusting a knob on the eyepiece, while he put on the appropriate range by a knob underneath. Three ranges were provided on this periscope: up to 1,000 metres for the machine-gun; 3,600 metres for armour-piercing shot, and 2,100 for high explosive. A rubber eye guard and brow pad were provided to protect the gunner from the lurching of the tank, but they were not efficient light excluders, and it is clear that sighting either of the turret guns by means of the periscope must have been a fairly chastening experience.

However, the more accurate method of laying the gun was by the alternative telescope sight. This was a straight-tube, moving eyepiece telescope, giving a magnification of x 2.5, and a field of view of just over 14 degrees. Like the periscope, it had an illuminated graticule with a hand-adjusted knob controlling three range scales, though these offered more scope than was available on the periscope. They showed up to 5,000 metres for high explosive, and 1,400 for the machine-gun. The telescope, however, shared a serious disadvantage with the periscope: its rubber eyeguard was not good at keeping out light, which must have hampered quick laying of the gun.

Each turret gun could be fired by hand or foot. For foot firing, the gunner sat with his toes resting on two sprung pedals mounted on either side of a pillar bolted to the gun mounting – the 76.2mm pedal on the left and the machine-gun on the right. On the other side of the turret, the loader could also fire the machine-gun if necessary by a hand-trigger on the gun, while there was also a hand-trigger on the main 76.2mm armament for the gunner-commander.

This latter hand-trigger was important, for the commander of the T-34 was a very overworked man. Since the driver had a very restricted field of view – and that directly to his front – the commander, using his throat microphone, had to direct him rather more precisely than in some Western tanks where the driver could see more. In addition, of course, the commander was entirely responsible for seeing that the rounds he fired from either of his guns hit the target.

Thus, gabbling his orders to the driver to get the tank positioned properly, shouting to the loader the kind of ammunition he had decided to fire, ducking down to the telescope to lay the gun, working out the range and opening fire – and then shrugging himself well clear of the 76.2mm as it smashed back for the full fourteen inches of its recoil – he had little time to see what any other tank was doing. Yet if he was troop commander, with three or more tanks under him, he could only tell his subordinates of his intentions by waving coloured flags, since wireless was not provided at lower command levels in Russian tank formations. Thus, by using the hand-trigger instead of the foot-button, he could at least keep himself in the upper part of the turret for longer at a time.

The commander was further hampered by two minor but troublesome design faults in the turret itself. First, the large access hatch on the turret roof hinged forward directly in front of his face, revealing his head and shoulders to flank sniper fire which killed many tank commanders – and also forcing him to peer round its

French Char B of 1940

Stalingrad 1942: German Mark IV with long 7.5cm gun

bulk to see what was happening in front. Second, the turret had a pronounced overhang at the rear, making an awkward, ledge-like space between it and the hull. German infantry soon learned to take advantage of the overworked commander's preoccupation with his gunlaying to approach the tank from behind, climb on the rear, wedge a time-fused tellermine into the overhang, and jump off. This accounts for German propaganda photographs issued early in the campaign showing T-34s with their turrets blown off – something which no contemporary standard German anti-tank gun was capable of doing.

Obviously, an electrical power traverse for the turret was highly desirable for the commander-gunner, and the T-34 designers provided one which gave a reasonably quick 360-degree traverse in just under 14 seconds. Faults could and did develop in this system, however, forcing the commander-gunner to haul the heavy turret round by a hand traverse. When this happened, he faced new

problems. The handwheel handle of the traverse was not pivotally mounted on the wheel, and it was very awkward to use when the turret had to be traversed quickly. It was very badly placed, being too far back for the left hand to work it easily. This meant adopting an awkward crouching position, using the right hand across the body, while straining to keep the head firmly pressed against the eyepiece of the telescope.

The turret offered design problems for the loader, too. The T-34 carried 77 rounds for the 76.2mm gun – an average break-down being 19 rounds of armour-piercing shot, 53 rounds of high explosive, and 5 of shrapnel. Of this total, however, only 9 rounds were easily accessible: 6 in racks at the left-hand wall of the fighting compartment, and 3 on the right. The remaining 68 rounds were distributed in eight metal bins at the bottom of the turret. These were covered by rubber matting and in fact formed the turret floor. Thus in any action where more than a handful of rounds was fired without an appreciable pause, the loader had to start uncovering and dismantling the turret floor in order to replenish the gun – no easy task since every time the 76.2mm gun fired, a very hot shell case was added to the tangle of bins and disturbed matting down below.

It can be seen that the T-34 was a long way from being a perfect tank. Design faults of the kind listed above were, of course, shared by several Western tanks: the heavy French Char B of 1940, for example, had a similar two-man turret, and the British Infantry Tank Mark I of 1939 – forerunner of the Matilda – reached new depths of commander discomfort by having only one man in the turret. All these faults, however, were basically minor in character. They could become of decisive importance *only* if the tanks which met the T-34 in battle were equal to it in more fundamental respects. The fundamentals of a tank are armament, armour, mobility. It is the degree of success in balancing these three factors which ultimately decides the fighting qualities of the tank. In each of these three factors, the T-34 offered the most formidable challenge of any tank in general service in its day.

Taking mobility first, let us examine the basic performance figures which emerged after the marathon winter trials. They were startingly good – a power-weight ratio of 17.9 brake horse-power per ton, and a top speed of 32 miles per hour. The power-weight equation is vital to the evaluation of the tank as a vehicle, since it reveals, irrespective of the weight of the tank or the size of its engine, the degree of efficiency reached in balancing these two vital considerations. Thus the T-34, producing nearly 18 horse-power for every ton of weight, stands high beside any tank in history. The contemporary German Mark III tank had a power-weight ratio, in its later versions, of about 14 horse-power per ton; the British Matilda of 7.2; the American Sherman of around 14.

As regards armour, the T-34 was by no means the best protected tank of its day – but it was by far the thickest-armoured of anything approaching its speed and range. The maximum thickness on the cast turret was 45mm on the early models. The hull – which was all-welded of rolled plate – was thinner, though the hardness of the armour was considered to be somewhat better than that of contemporary British plate. These armour thicknesses were swiftly increased after the first taste of battle in 1941, soon reaching 65mm on the turret and 47mm on the hull.

Perhaps the best point of the T-34's armour was that it was sloped and angled. This was a technique to which neither British nor German tank designers yet paid much attention. Sloped armour greatly increased the protection which the T-34 gave against conventional armour-piercing projectiles. Ballistic tests have since shown how far-sighted the Koshkin team was in this respect. For instance, a steel plate 100mm thick, if sloped at sixty degrees to the vertical, is equivalent to a vertical plate about 300mm thick, though the equation differs to some extent, depending on the nature of the impacting projectile. The nose armour of the T-34, in fact, was sloped at exactly sixty degrees.

However, it was in the third vital consideration – the gun – that the T-34 really asserted its superiority. The 1940 model of the 76.2mm gun, 41.2 calibres long, which became its standard equipment, had a muzzle velocity of 2,172 feet per second – roughly that of the 75mm gun on the American Sherman which was to go into general service nearly two years later, and very much better than the 1,300 feet per second of the short 75mm gun on the German Mark IV. This machine was still only appearing in small numbers, and was Germany's heaviest-gunned tank.

Thus the arming by the Russians of a fast medium tank with a gun of the penetrating power of the 76.2mm went far to render the whole of Germany's tank force obsolete from the moment

Above: Commander's discomfort: The British one-man turret Infantry Tank Mark I: France 1940. *Below:* Infantry Tank Mark II Matilda, as used by Red Army in infantry support role

that the T-34 was met in battle. Britain, too, was left far behind, stranded between the pre-war faith in the light tank which had been severely eroded by the event of 1940, and the even more traditional concept of the infantry tank, like the Valentine or Matilda, both still armed with the two-pounder gun. British and American tanks which were soon to be delivered to Russia by sea and by the Persian land route were regarded by Soviet soldiers as not up to standard for the Russian front, though the thickly-armoured Matilda was sometimes used in a purely infantry-support role.

Until the T-34 was revealed to the Germany army in the opening days of Operation *Barbarossa* the German Mark III had been regarded by the tank experts of the world as the queen of the armoured battlefield. It was certainly an advanced tank for its time, but by 1941 its time was nearly over. Some of its features now showed that those responsible for German tank production had allowed the runaway victory of 1940 to lull them into complacence. The vital statistics of this, the main German battle tank in the invasion of Russia, reveal the shock which was coming.

The Mark III had been ordered in 1935, and began to be produced in small numbers of 1936. Its first major production type, the *Ausfuhrung F*, appeared in 1940. This model had a battle-weight of a little over 20 tons, a road speed of 25 miles per hour, and maximum armour of 30mm on both hull and turret. As we have seen, the power-weight ratio was around 14 horse-power to the ton, and the effective range of the tank was less than half that of the T-34. This was a highly-important factor for armour operating in difficult conditions over the largely-destroyed Russian road system. The Mark III (F) carried 70 gallons of fuel, giving it a range, by road, of about 100 miles – compared with the 135 gallons and 280 miles of the T-34.

The difference in armament was even more marked than that in automotive performance. The Mark III (F) was originally equipped with the 37mm gun – little more than a toy when pitted against the armour of the T-34. However, in general, by the time the invasion of Russia began, the Mark III had been up-gunned, though with another inadequate weapon. This was a 50mm gun, but the version was a short one only 42 calibres long, with a low muzzle velocity and hence a poor performance against armour.

This was the result of an astonishing lapse by the German armaments authorities. Hitler, who always had an alert technical eye where his panzers were concerned, had earlier ordered that when the Mark III was up-gunned, it should receive in its turret the long-barrelled L60 50mm gun, and not the short L42. However, in an ill-chosen act of independence, the German army ordnance office decided to disobey, and chose the shorter gun . . . a decision, von Mellenthin remarked gloomily, which 'went far to lose us the war . . .' At a tank demonstration a few weeks before he launched *Barbarossa*, Hitler noticed that his orders had been flouted. He was furious. Guderian, who was present during the Fuhrer's explosion of rage, recorded that even years later Hitler 'was to refer to this disobedient inefficiency whenever an attempt was made to defend the army ordnance office in his presence . . .'

It was too late to change the Mark III in time for *Barbarossa*. Most of the tanks to be used in the invasion had, of course, been issued to units, and they mounted the L42. The German tank force which drove into Russia in June 1941 contained 2,068 Mark IIIs out of a total of 3,200 German tanks. Of these Mark IIIs, 131 were still armed with the 37mm gun, 1,893 with the L42 short 50mm, and only 44 with the long L60 50mm. Thus the bulk of the panzer force was equipped with an inadequate weapon.

Neither side realised, before *Bar-*

Above: German soldiers examine T-34/76s. *Right:* Outclassed: the German Mark III with the short 5cm gun

barossa, how clearly ahead the Russians were in the field of basic tank design. In the spring of 1941, Hitler, possibly in an effort to convince the Russians that a German attack on them was not in his mind, ordered that a Russian military commission should be shown over German tank schools and factories, and that nothing should be hidden from them. The outcome startled the panzer officers who showed them round. The Russian delegation remained firmly unconvinced that the Mark IV could possibly be Germany's heaviest tank, and complained bitterly that Hitler's order that they should see everything was not being carried out. Gradually it dawned on the puzzled Germans that the Russians themselves must possess more formidable tanks than had been imagined. 'It was at the end of July 1941,' a panzer general wryly reported later, 'that the T-34 tank appeared at the front and the riddle of the new Russian model was solved . . .'

On any comparison of the T-34 with the Mark III, its principal German adversary in 1941, the balance must be seen to tip decisively in favour of the Russian tank. The T-34 had better armour, a better gun, longer range, higher speed, and better economy in the use of fuel. Against this, its two-man turret was poor and cramped, compared with the comparatively spacious three-man fighting compartment of the Mark III. The German tanks were better equipped with radio, and their engineering was more sophisticatedly finished – though here, too, it seems that Russian factories managed to concentrate successfully on essentials.

A T-34 was examined in great detail by the British School of Tank Technology during the war. Its report on the engine noted that 'the quality of the workmanship varies considerably. Whilst the highly-stressed parts have a finish comparable with that of British aero engines of moderate output, the sand castings by contrast are exceptionally rough. In spite of this, however, the latter appear to be sound, there being no sign of porosity or blow holes on the manufactured surfaces. Most of the important bolts

and studs are stress-relieved and ground, and on a few components the standard of finish is very high. The large number of inspection stamps on certain components is very noticeable . . .'

This British evaluation of the T-34 is important today, because it judged the tank by contemporary technological standards, and not with the benefit of hindsight. Its final verdict was an implicit tribute to Koshkin and his team, as men who concentrated only on the absolute essentials of tank design, but who were exceptionally clear-headed as to what those essentials were:

'The design shows a clear appreciation of the essentials of an effective tank and the requirements of war, duly adjusted to the particular characteristics of the Russian soldier, the terrain, and the manufacturing facilities available. When it is considered how recently Russia has become industrialised, and how great a proportion of the industrial regions have been overrun by the enemy . . . the design and production of such useful tanks in such great numbers stands out as an engineering achieve-

ment of the first magnitude . . .'

Thus, when the Germans struck, the Koshkin design team had provided Russia with an armoured instrument which was technically capable of frustrating the panzers. It was not yet present in enormous numbers: by June there were 1,110 T-34s in the Soviet tank park, but they had not begun to arrive at their battalions until late spring, and they were scattered throughout the five Soviet military districts. Nevertheless, had they been concentrated into one formidable, well-led striking force, they were probably sufficient to have blunted the panzer onslaught.

The operative words here are 'well-led'. The Russian command was now to find out that the possession of a weapon is not decisive unless its possessor knows how to use it. The question during the agonised summer of 1941 was whether the German panzers would give the Russians time to learn. The T-34 in the hands of *Stavka*, the Russian supreme headquarters, was still a rapier in the hands of a novice. This, too, was a situation which had its roots in the immediate past.

31

Russian theories of war

A decade before Operation *Barbarossa*, the theories of mobile mechanised war had gripped the imagination of Russian commanders even more tightly than had been the case in Germany – and much more so than in the military establishments of Britain and the United States. For this, Russia could thank the first of her great post-Revolution soldiers, Mikhail Tukhachevsky, a former lieutenant of the Imperial Russian Army, who had caught Trotsky's eye in 1918 and later successfully commanded a Red army against the White troops of Admiral Kolchak. Brilliantly professional, proud, impulsive, and cruel, Tukhachevsky believed in the cult of the non-stop offensive, and he saw clearly that the fast tank was the weapon for his purpose. He envisaged, remarkably accurately, total war – a conflict which would embrace the entire national life.

By 1930, Tukhachevsky was forming the first mechanised brigades of the Red Army. These were based loosely on the all-tank ideas put forward in Britain by Hobart and Fuller. A mechanised brigade consisted largely of tanks: a normal establishment being three battalions of the fast BT models which were now coming off the production lines, with a small infantry battalion equipped with automatic weapons and various small auxiliary units. Tukhachevsky had now gathered round him a group of like-minded officers – men like Uborevitch, Yakir, Khalepski, and Alksnis – who played their part in the creation, in 1932, of the first Russian mechanised corps. This was intended for the role of mechanised strategic cavalry, and was an instrument of formidable striking power. A mechanised corps, Tukhachevsky-style, was made up of either two or three mechanised brigades (each of about one hundred tanks), with a lorried infantry brigade and a mechanised field artillery regiment. Such a formation, while it was less powerful than Guderian's classic conception of the panzer division, bore a remarkable resemblance to some of the highly-effective battle groups which the Wehrmacht assembled on an ad hoc basis during the Second World War.

Meanwhile, the infantry support role of the tank was not neglected, and two further systems of using armour were devised for the Red Army. Each infantry division was given a tank battalion – usually equipped with T-26s – and in addition, both army and corps headquarters had independent tank brigades attached for use as needed. These brigades each comprised three battalions of light or medium tanks – T-26s or T-28s, with an occasional battalion of heavy T-35s.

The running of three such lavish systems was possible only because the scale of armoured development

Marshal Budyenny

Marshal Voroshilov

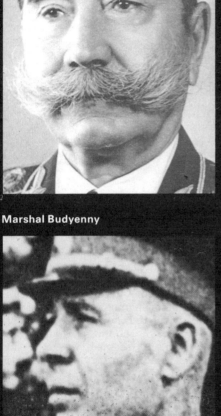

Marshal Timoshenko

Marshal Zhukov

was prodigious: by 1935 Russia possessed 7,000 tanks, 100,000 military lorries, and 150,000 general purpose tractors. However, in Russia as farther west, the supporters of mechanisation faced a hostile cavalry lobby. The members of this cavalry clique were often veterans of the First Cavalry Army of 1919, which was commanded by Marshal Semyon Budenny, a former cavalry NCO, with men like Timoshenko, Klimenti Voroshilov, and Georgi Zhukov as his subordinates. These cavalrymen basked in Stalin's approval, and because he resented Tukhachevsky's implicit divorce of the Red Army from political interests, he used them to counter the growing influence of the military progressives. These Russian cavalrymen were not necessarily hidebound traditionalists: in particular, Zhukov would soon prove that he was a master of the armoured set-piece battle on the Montgomery model. But at a vital time in the last half of the decade, their influence would be disastrous, because they, almost alone, were to survive the great purge which crippled the Red Army between 1937 and 1938.

The reasons for the purge are not the province of this account: Stalin imagined, rightly or wrongly, that the high officers of the Red Army could be a threat to his position. Instantly they were swept away. In April 1937 the political commissar system, which had fallen into disuse earlier, was brought back into the army. From now forward, troops could not be moved nor orders issued without an accompanying political signature. On 9th June, accused of treason, Tukhachevsky, Uborevitch and Yakir were removed from command; on 11th June they were tried by a special military court; at dawn on the 12th they were shot. They were followed, over the next few months, by the greater part of the officer corps, executed or sent to labour camps. Nine out of ten of all generals vanished: eight out of ten of all colonels.

The cavalry clique survived to inherit the vacant commands. There was an immediate reaction against the 'bourgeois' ideas of Western tank theorists. The mechanised corps were disbanded, and their units were distributed among the infantry commands. The tank, it seemed, was to return to its traditional role of infantry support. Tanks, of course, were still held in vast numbers. There were estimated to be 24,000 machines in the Soviet tank park by 1941, though by then the bulk of this force was becoming obsolescent.

It was an irony of military history that at this stage, after Tukhachevsky and his friends had been destroyed, Russian tank designers had finally succeeded in making available for the Red Army the two basic tanks needed to keep it ahead of the rest of the world. These were the dual-purpose T-34 itself, which could be used in either a cavalry or an infantry-support role, and also a

further new tank, of a heavier type. This was the 46-ton KV-I, which used the same engine as the T-34 and was thus, in view of its greater weight, much slower, with a maximum speed of about 24 miles per hour. The KV-I was also armed with the T-34's 76.2mm gun. Its armour was considerably thicker, fitting for a set-piece battle role. On the turret, it reached 75mm. This made it roughly equal in this respect to the British Matilda, which had given Rommel's 7th Panzer Division an unpleasant shock at Arras in May 1940.

Between them, these two tanks provided the Russian command with all that it needed for basic tank warfare. Production problems on both models had been simplified, since they shared many components of gun and engine. This, alone, was a tremendous advantage in campaigning conditions.

Yet with these tools at its disposal, the Russian command floundered, while indecisive arguments raged

Russian KV-1 heavy tank: 46 tons, 76.2mm gun

about their use. The sad Russian experience in Finland, however, coupled with the spectacular German panzer successes in France, swung opinion back towards the theories of a strategic role for mechanised forces. A start was made on the reorganisation of the armoured force, beginning with the establishment of tank divisions on the new German model. Each of these divisions was intended to consist of two tank regiments, one lorried infantry regiment, and an artillery regiment. The total tank establishment was about 400 tanks. These were a mixture of BTs, T-34s, and KV-Is. A larger formation, the tank corps, comprised two tank divisions and one lorried infantry division. It was planned to have no fewer than twenty tank corps, containing forty tank divisions, by the autumn of 1941.

Paper plans, however, are a very different thing from trained military units. The crews to man such a vast force were no longer there. Not unnaturally, in view of the terrified paralysis which had gripped Russian unit commanders since the great purge, the state of tank crew training, even on the older machines, was now abysmal. Tactical training was virtually non-existent. The official Soviet history states frankly that of the entire Soviet tank park, just over a quarter of the machines were in working order, and that the new generation of tank crews had only a very rudimentary knowledge of their job.

'The training of specialists for the new tanks,' says this account, 're-quired a consideryble time. Since there was a shortage of tank crews, it was necessary to transfer to the tank units officers, soldiers and sergeants from other army formations – from infantry and cavalry units. By the beginning of the war, many tank men had only one-and-a-half to two hours' experience in actual driving. Even many officers in tank units were not fully qualified to command them . . .'

The actual supply of the new T-34s to the armoured units was also hopelessly in arrears. Few of the new mechanised formations had anything like a full complement of the new tanks when the Germans struck. In the XIV Mechanised Corps, stationed in the vital Western Military District commanded by General Pavlov – shot by a revengeful Stalin after he had failed to stem the panzer tide – the situation was appalling. On paper, the corps' establishment of tanks was 1,025, of which 420 should have been T-34s and 126 KV-Is. In other words, this was intended to be an exceptionally powerful corps, with three tank divisions instead of two. The reality

Above left: KV-1 supports Russian assault troops as they move forward.
Left: Motorised confusion: a German mobile column crossroads

was very different. There was a total force of 508 obsolescent BT tanks. Even these machines did not begin to arrive at units until the end of April.

Behind the vast, largely obsolete Russian tank park and its ill-trained crews and demoralised commanders, the infrastructure of a mechanised army was also grossly inadequate. Things had changed since Tukhachevsky's day. There was a severe shortage of motor transport, and much of the military supply system was being operated by ancient lorries or even horse-drawn transport – though the latter anachronism was one which was shared by the German army throughout the war.

Even allowing for all this, however, the task facing the German armies as they began Operation *Barbarossa* was immense. The Battle of France had been a panzer gamble, and a successful one. The Russian adventure had built-in risks which dwarfed it. In numbers of tanks, the Russians were greatly superior, and they also enjoyed the limited qualitative superiority conferred by more than 1,000 T-34s and nearly 400 KVs. In relation to this force, and to the size of its geographical task, the German tank force was absurdly small. Against these disadvantages stood the superlatively-good training of the German tank crews, and the backwardness of their Russian counterparts. Both sides had fine human material – men who would fight until they dropped and who could stand up to the cruel rigours of modern war. The Germans needed a swift, obliterating victory; the Russians needed time. In this struggle, the T-34, from the opening weeks of the campaign, was to play a vital part. Its first effect was moral rather than material. It was to give the panzer crews a shock – the first real shock they had sustained in almost two years of successful war.

The first clash

It had been a long hot day for the German tanks of 17th Panzer Division, edging slowly forward through the patchwork of potato crops and corn-fields around Senno, in front of the Dniepr river. Here and there, columns of oily black smoke rose from the smouldering grain or scrub, marking the last fight of a light Russian T-26 or of a German Mark III. The German armour, outrunning its supply eche-lons in the onward rush since it had launched Operation *Barbarossa* seven-teen days before, was short of ammunition. Just as the tired gun-ners, crouched in their hot, reeking turrets, had received orders to cut down the amount of gunfire, a single Russian tank with a squat unfamiliar silhouette emerged from the corn. Several German tanks engaged it – and watched their shots ricochet away from its massive turret. The Russian tank swung along a farm track, at the end of which waited a standard 37mm anti-tank gun. The German crew pumped shells at the oncoming tank until it reached their position, pivoted on its wide tracks, and crushed the gun into the ground. Leaving a burning Mark III behind it, it lum-bered on into the German rear for more than nine miles, until eventually it was destroyed from behind by a shot from a 100mm gun. Such was 17th Panzer Division's first glimpse of a T-34. The date was 8th July, 1941.

This incident on the banks of the Dniepr was being repeated at various points all along the Eastern Front in the opening days of *Barbarossa*. Contact with the T-34 was proving to be a traumatic experience for German tank crews whose morale, at least in part, had been built on the confident assumption of German technical superiority. 'A wonder weapon,' one German account called the new tank, '... spreading terror and fear wherever it moved ...' Meanwhile, the German

German Mark IIIs outside Kharkov, 1941, with Hanomag command half-track vehicle

infantry quickly found a sardonic name for the standard 37mm anti-tank gun. They called it 'the army's door-knocker.'

The T-34's heavier companion, the KV-I, also caused consternation. The 1st Panzer Division, in Leeb's Army Group North, met it three days after the invasion. The division's own account tells the story:

'Our companies opened fire at about 800 yards but it was ineffective. We moved closer and closer to the enemy, who for his part continued to approach us unconcerned. Very soon we were facing each other at 50 to 100 yards. A fantastic exchange of fire took place without any visible German success. The Russian tanks continued to advance and all armour-piercing

shells simply bounced off them. Thus we were soon faced with the alarming situation of the Russian tanks driving through the tanks of 1st Panzer Regiment towards our own infantry and rear areas. Our panzer regiment therefore about-turned and drove back with the KV-Is . . . roughly in line with them. In the course of that operation we succeeded in immobilising some of them with special purpose shells at very close range – 30 to 60 yards . . .'

Yet, even allowing for the technological shock which the Germans had sustained, the extent of foreboding concerning the new Russian tanks seems excessive, when viewed against the appalling Russian situation shown on the battle maps in the summer of 1941. On the day that 17th Panzer Division met the T-34 outside Senno, the Germans appeared to be racing to a victory even more startling, even more complete, than that of 1940. Three army groups had opened the offensive: South, under

Below: The 'door-knocker' German 3.7cm anti-tank gun. Behind it a captured T-34. *Above left:* In the wake of the panzers: a burning Russian village. *Below left:* On wide tracks T-34s advance through the snow

Field-Marshal Ritter von Leeb

Field-Marshal Wernher von Bock

Field-Marshal Gerd von Rundstedt

Field-Marshal Albert Kesselring

Rundstedt; Centre, under Bock, and North, under Leeb. By July 8th, Army Group Centre alone had captured more than 300,000 Russians, and destroyed or captured 2,500 tanks and 1,500 guns. The booty was enormous, and the panzers were pressing on: by July 11th Guderian's Second Panzer Group was crossing the Dniepr, capturing Smolensk five days later.

'On this day,' wrote Guderian proudly, 'I was decorated with the Oak Leaves to the Knight's Cross. I was the fifth man in the army, and the twenty-fourth in all the armed forces, to receive this decoration . . .'

Already, however, the shadows were beginning to fall. By the beginning of August, the sheer geographical immensity of the task was still daunting. The panzer force, which had now fought a longer campaign than any armoured force had yet done in the history of war, was showing signs of mechanical disintegration. The whole situation was being made worse by the peculiarly effective way in which even tactically defeated Russian armies fought.

Hitler's Directive No. 21, which had given the outline plan for *Barbarossa*, was uncompromisingly a tank operation. Its success depended entirely on the speed with which it could be carried out. 'The bulk of the Russian army stationed in Western Russia,' said the directive, 'will be destroyed by daring operations led by deeply penetrating armoured spearheads. Russian forces still capable of giving battle will be prevented from withdrawing into the depths of Russia . . .'

For such an operation, the vastness of the Russian spaces appeared to offer a tempting panzer battleground – yet it was this very vastness, more than anything else, which gave the Russians their chance. This Russian advantage was compounded by the fact that the German tank force was not technically suitable, nor sufficiently numerous, for the task it had been set. Indeed, it could be argued that if Hitler had been able to deploy 2,000 T–34s instead of 2,000 Mark IIIs for the invasion of Russia, the history of the world have been changed. For the technically-superior Russian tanks, even badly handled, could inflict heavy casualties on the shrinking total of panzers. The German general Erich von Manstein, who commanded a panzer corps in Leeb's Army Group North, reflected later that:

'. . . It goes without saying that the further a single panzer corps – or, indeed, the entire panzer group – ventured into the depth of the Russian hinterland, the greater the hazards became . . . It may be said that the safety of a tank formation operating in the enemy's rear depends upon its ability to keep moving. Once it comes to a halt it will be immediately assailed from all sides by the enemy's reserves . . .'

In Russia, however, the enemy's 'reserves' were frequently not the ordered formations held back by an intelligent commander in accordance with classical theories of war, but formidable, unpredictable bands of determined men grouped around a handful of T–34s or KVs, who had been surrounded a day or so before, and were now trying to break out of the tenuous noose that the panzers had spun. This situation repeated itself constantly. The first part of Hitler's Directive No. 21 was working out, but not the second. In successive encirclement battles, Russian army after Russian army was surrounded and technically destroyed. Again and again, however, the steel cord formed by the panzers was too thin to stop tens of thousands of Russian soldiers from breaking through and filtering east. By any conventional military standard, the Russian forces were out-thought, out-manoeuvred, and beaten. But the Russian soldier had read no books about war. In his encircled enclaves, he fought on and on, sucking the scanty German panzers into new whirlpools of battle, holding back the German tanks that

should have been reinforcing the drive east. By September, the German command estimated Russian losses at 2,500,000 men, 18,000 tanks, and 14,000 aircraft. Already, however, the German command was realising that it had been over-confident. The OKH chief of staff, Halder, remarked ruefully in a diary entry: 'We underestimated Russia. We reckoned with 200 divisions, but we have already identified 360 . . .'

The panzers' problem was seen clearly by Field-Marshal Albert Kesselring, who at this time commanded *Luftflotte 2*. His personal flights over the Russian plains and forests at the controls of his Focke-Wulf·189 gave him, perhaps, a clearer geographical perspective than was available to the panzer commanders on the ground. He assessed the fatal flaw in the plan to defeat Russia with the existing German tank force, however brilliantly it was handled:

Left: In the bag: Russian prisoners, exhausted, wait for the prison camp.
Below: Over the marshes: German infantry attack

'Our strategic mechanised forces had to be proportionate to the depth and breadth of the area to be conquered, and to the strength of the enemy, and we had not anywhere near this strength. Our fully tracked vehicles, including tanks, were not adequately serviceable. There were technical limits to constant movement. A mobile operation in 1,000 kilometres depth through strongly-occupied territory requires vast supplies, especially if there is no chance of falling back on large and useful enemy stores. Our lines of communication and our airfields lay mostly in enemy-threatened country, and were insufficiently protected . . .'

The Russian command was well aware that the panzers faced a problem, but it also faced a gigantic crisis of its own. Its armies, corps and divisions were at a fraction of their proper strength, and the Russian tank park had virtually been swept away. In the factories in Leningrad and the Urals, the T-34s were coming off the lines in increasing numbers. Almost 3,000 were produced in 1941, but many of the crews who could have manned them were already dead or herded into German prison camps.

Clearly, the reconstructed mechanised corps was an absurdly ambitious unit for the depleted and largely untrained Russian tank force. There was now a return to the independent tank brigade. Each of these brigades, in theory, had a tank regiment with three small mixed tank battalions, a lorried machine-gun battalion, and a company each of anti-tank guns and mortars. In practice, even these small formations at this time rarely reached their full establishment. Soon the average tank brigade was down to a tank strength of under fifty machines, contained in two tank battalions of around twenty-three tanks each. These smaller units were better suited to the capabilities of Russian armoured commanders as they strove to relearn their jobs in the middle of a campaign, and they

Left: How Kesselring saw the front: the Focke-Wulf 189. *Above:* T-34 with back of turret blown off – possibly by mine wedged under overhang. *Below:* Production goes on: later models of T34/76 at a Urals factory

Defending the capital : T-34s and BTs

could also quickly be moved to plug a gap in a crumbling defence system. Moreover, they were composed almost entirely of T-34s, since this was now accounting for almost all Soviet tank production. The T-34 was inflicting losses which the German factories were finding it difficult to replace.

While the Russian factories in 1941 were producing their 3,000 T-34s and some hundreds of KVs, German production was falling behind. The estimated production of Mark IIIs for January 1942, for instance, was an unsatisfactory 190 machines – but only 159 were actually built. With the Mark III's eagerly-awaited successor, the Mark IV, the picture was worse. There were 531 Mark IVs in service when the campaign opened. Nine months later, on 1st April 1942, there were 552. Production was barely keeping pace with campaign losses.

It is interesting to note that even after its stupefying losses, the Red Army, in terms of machines, was more than holding its own in relation to the German invasion forces. When Zhukov finally began the Moscow counter-offensive in December 1941, it was only, paradoxically, in men that the Russians were lagging, for they had lost many millions in killed, wounded, and captured since June. They had, of course, also lost their enormous margin of machine super-

iority, but the best available figures give them almost 2,000 tanks against 1,500 German: 3,600 aircraft against 2,500 German: but only 4,190,000 troops available against 5,000,000 German.

However, the figures for Russian tank and aircraft production represented the achievements of the first nine months of the year. In the .autumn, as the great industrial regions were seized by the German armies, the factories had been torn from their sites and bodily transported east. This interruption in production sent output plummetting in the last quarter of 1941. The great Kirov plant moved from Leningrad to Chelybinsk, and was rebuilt there alongside the even bigger tank pro-

ducing plant evacuated from Kharkov. This complex became known as Tankograd, producing heavy tanks like the KV series and later the Josef Stalin model. The T-34 itself was produced at a centre in the Urals known as Uralmashzavod, which consisted of part of the evacuated Kharkov plant grafted on to the original Urals factory at Nizhniy Tagil. Prodigious efforts were made to get this plant back into production as quickly as possible. According to the official Soviet history, the last batch of workers left Kharkov for the Urals on 19th October. By 8th December, the first consignment of T-34s had been produced. They were hurried to the front.

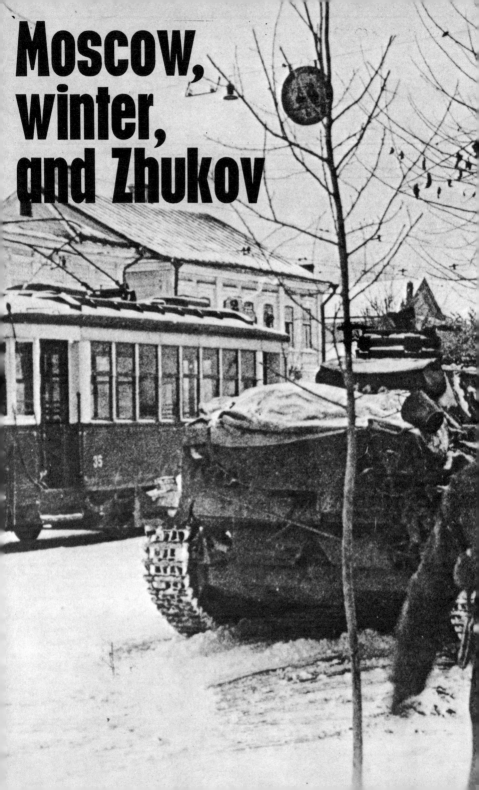

Moscow, winter, and Zhukov

The successful defence of Moscow by the Red Army was one of the great turning points of the war. Curiously, however, the part played by the Russian soldier in this triumph has been somewhat discounted: mud and then frost, it is often said, defeated the German panzers. Winter was the enemy, aided by the sad mistakes of the Führer. This theory has gained momentum because far more German commanders than Russian have written their memoirs: Manstein, Guderian, Mellenthin, von Senger, Halder have all been translated into English, while Kleist, Blumenthal and others have poured out their hearts in articles and recorded conversations with British and American commentators. On the Russian side, Zhukov and Chuikov are almost alone with major accounts in English – and both books have been strained to fit the Party mould.

However, when the defence of Moscow is looked at from the Russian side of the hill, the picture is significantly different. The German defeat appears to a much greater extent to be both a strategic failure by Hitler and a tactical failure by the panzer leaders. This crucial tactical failure, moreover, occurred because the German panzers, on the edge of triumph, were critically mauled by the new Russian tanks.

Looking at the strategic failure first, it can be seen that it was twofold. First, and most important, was the basic over-estimation of the capabilities of the German panzer force for the whole Russian operation. This error, as we shall see, was compounded by the conditions of the Russian autumn and winter, but it might well have been decisive even if Russia had basked in eternal summer. The second part of the strategic error was a decision by Hitler himself.

The Führer's hopes were high as the

German Mark III in Kalinin: November 1941

Artillery target: devastated German
column outside Moscow, 15th December
1941

panzers rolled forward into the hot
and dusty plains. By 16th July,
advancing at a fantastic average of
twenty miles a day, they were two-
thirds of the way to Moscow. At this
point, Hitler switched them to other
objectives. With Army Group Centre
at Smolensk, Army Group North
cutting off Leningrad, and Army
Group South driving on Kiev, he
turned the two great panzer groups of
Army Group Centre to the wing Army
Groups, ordering Guderian's Second
Panzer Group to encircle the Russians
round Kiev, and Hoth's Third to
assist in the isolation of Leningrad.
He intended in this way to accomplish
both the piecemeal destruction of the
Russian armies, and the capture and
elimination of vital industrial areas.

His Directive No. 34, issued on 21st
August, insisted that 'the principal
objects that must be achieved ...
before the onset of winter, are not the
capture of Moscow but rather, in the
south, the occupation of the Crimea

and the industrial and coal region of
the Donetz, together with the isolation of the Russian oil region in the
Caucasus, and, in the north, the
encirclement of Leningrad and
junction with the Finns ...'

The OKH Chief of Staff, Halder, was
swift to condemn the new plan. He
confided to his diary that it implied
'a shift of our strategy from the
operational to the tactical level. If
striking at small concentrations
becomes our sole objective, the campaign will resolve itself into a series
of minor successes which will advance
our front only by inches. Pursuing
such a policy eliminates all tactical
risks and enables us gradually to
close the gaps between the fronts of
the army groups, but the result will
be that we feed all our strength into
a front expanding in width at the
sacrifice of depth, and end up with
position warfare ...' Guderian, too,
wrote later that 'these manoeuvres on
our part simply gave the Russians
time to set up new formations and to
use their inexhaustible manpower ...'

Halder's reference to the elimination of 'tactical risks' is significant,

and is perhaps the best justification of Hitler's move. For by normal military standards, the Führer's ideas were not wrong. The apparent triumphant advance of Army Group Centre was becoming open, on its flanks, to decisive counter-attack: even badly-organised Russian armour could inflict grievous casualties, as will soon be seen. The Germans could not go on forever as though the Russian tanks did not exist. Zhukov, who was now to conduct the defence of Moscow with exemplary energy, determination and skill had no difficulty in understanding Hitler's move. He noted:

'As far as the temporary halt of the drive towards Moscow in August is concerned, the Germans had no choice but to divert part of their forces to the operations in the Ukraine. Without those operations, the central group of the German forces might have been in an even less favourable situation: the Soviet Supreme Headquarters reserves that were thrown into operational gaps in the southwest in September would otherwise have been used against the flank and rear of Army Group Centre during its drive against Moscow . . .'

What Directive No. 34 did show was that Hitler had not fully grasped the nature of Operation *Barbarossa*: that it was a panzer gamble in which Moscow, the seat of the rigid, authoritarian administration, was an unusually desirable prize. Even as early as September, it was becoming clear that the gamble, for all the stunning local successes, had failed, that the choice was between withdrawal to a safer line where communications would be easier, or to tackle the Russian reserves and the Russian winter in a hopelessly extended position. Only one of German's leading soldiers steadily advocated withdrawal during the coming weeks. He was the skilful, sagacious Rundstedt, and he was eventually rewarded by dismissal.

The German armies were held out of Leningrad by the stubborn defence of the city and its garrisons, but they won a shattering victory at Kiev, with the now-customary astronomical bag of men and booty. At this point, Hitler switched his strategy, and decided that the time was ripe to drive on Moscow. In fact, the time proved to be overripe. Although the panzers won another great victory at Viazma-Briansk, the broad black arrows showing the panzer progress on the map were now driving into winter. In addition, they were now beginning to make overconfident tactical errors which gave the painfully-learning Russian tank formations their chance.

The autumn was a bad time for the panzers. Before winter fully gripped the steppe, the roads and tracks would freeze and thaw at unpredictable intervals, so that ground which had appeared to be easily passable at dawn could be a quagmire at sunset creating great bogs of mud where the German tanks floundered helplessly. Such ground, however, was often negotiated without too much difficulty by the T-34s with their wide tracks –

55

Field-Marshal Keitel and Hitler

nineteen inches compared with the fourteen inches of the Mark III – and their high power-to-weight ratio. For the first time, as autumn deepened into winter, it was the Russians in their T-34s who were more mobile on tracks.

It was time for a Russian armoured counterstroke, even on a small scale. Such a stroke, in fact, could not be a big one, for as October began, there were only 383 Russian tanks on the whole of the Western Front. Yet it should be remembered that a great force was not necessary to rebuff a panzer attack. The number of German tanks leading an entire panzer group was not large. Even losses which seem statistically small could throw a whole advance out of gear, and seriously blunt the panzer edge. To do this, however, the Russian tank commanders had to learn new techniques. The decisive advantage which the panzers always possessed was the brave, intelligent quality of their unit leadership. If the T-34s were to

maul the Mark IIIs, even on a locally decisive scale, this must be matched by the Russians. Early in October, near Tula on the vulnerable front south of Moscow, it was so matched.

The Russian 4th Tank Brigade, commanded by Colonel M Katukov, had been scraped together by the Russian command from the precious T-34s which were scattered at various points along the front, and were also coming from the factories. It was even harder to find crews than tanks, and the eye of *Stavka* had finally fallen on the tank training school near Kharkov. The students and staff of this school manned Katukov's tanks, experienced tank men leavened with untried cadets. Early in October, Katukov's brigade was ordered to plug the gap round Tula, which was being threatened by Guderian's Second Panzer Group.

The van division of Guderian's panzer group was the 4th Panzer, commanded by General Freiherr von Langermann. This division had entered Orel on 3rd October, taking the Russians so much by surprise that its tanks drove through streets in which the electric trams were still running. Ahead lay stretches of open countryside for more than one hundred miles, to the suburbs of Moscow. Katukov and his tank school, in their handful of T-34s – about fifty, if the brigade was at normal strength – were the only Russian armour in Langermann's path.

Although the capture of Orel had been a rich dividend for panzer daring all was not well with 4th Panzer Division or its parent formation, the XXIV Panzer Corps. The corps commander, General Freiherr von Geyr, was calling desperately for petrol, since he was finding it difficult to capture enough to keep his tanks on the move. The airfield at Orel offered the opportunity to fly in fuel, and Guderian immediately requested that 100,000 gallons be brought as soon as possible. Petrol, however, was not all that was needed. Von Geyr's men were still shivering in the summer uniforms in which they had crossed the Russian frontier in June. Boots, socks, shirts were needed, but the roads were simply not adequate to get transport through. Few of the roads behind Orel were metalled – and even when they were it often meant little. The main one from Sevsk to Orel, said Guderian, 'consisted largely of one bomb crater after another . . . the state of traffic was appalling . . .' It was a fairly typical position for a panzer division at the beginning of October, and no better moment could have been found to hit it hard.

Katukov did not miss his opportunity. He had infantry under command, and he used rifle battalions to draw the panzers on. Then his T-34s nipped 4th Panzer in the flanks, to such good effect that more than thirty of Langermann's shrinking force of Mark IIIs and Mark IVs were left burning on the steppe. During the same night, the first snow fell, melting swiftly, leaving the cratered roads morasses of mud. On the broad tracks of the T-34s, Katukov safely withdrew his force. His casualties are not recorded, but Guderian, walking over the battle area three days later, counted the knocked out tanks and noted that 'the damage suffered by the Russians was considerably less than that to our tanks . . .' He added, sombrely: 'They are learning.'

The Mark IVs, in particular, were finding that the T-34 had a strong tactical edge in tank-versus-tank fighting. The short-barrelled 75mm gun in the German turret was only effective against the T-34 from the rear – and even then the Russian tank had to be hit on the engine grating to knock it out. This needed a cool head and a sharp eye, whereas almost any hit from the Russian 76.2mm gun would pierce and destroy either the Mark III or the Mark IV. 'Grievous casualties,' recorded the German group commander. 'The rapid advance which we planned had to be abandoned for the moment . . .'

Langermann, indeed, had to pause for two days. He moved forward again towards Mtensk on 11th October. The roads were so cratered and full of mud that 4th Panzer Division was strung out over more than fifteen miles when his leading tanks entered the burning town. Once more Katukov's T-34s appeared like ochre-coloured ghosts along the flank of the German column, cutting it into easily-digested lengths and wiping it out piecemeal. Within a few hours, Langermann's division was a broken formation. The German tank gunners, for their part, had found that the new Russian machines were not the sitting-duck BTs and T-28s of the earlier phase of the campaign. A panzer sergeant summed it up:

'. . . there is nothing more frightening than a tank battle against superior force. Numbers – they don't mean much, we were used to it. But better machines, that's terrible. You race the engine, but she responds too slowly. The Russian tanks are so agile, at close range they will climb a slope or cross a piece of swamp faster than

Above left: Waiting for the Stukas: a Soviet anti-aircraft unit. *Below left:* War in the forests: a white-dappled T-34 followed by infantry with machine carbines. *Above:* Outside Leningrad: German infantry wait in a captured trench, 1941

you can traverse the turret. And through the noise and the vibration you keep hearing the clang of shot against armour. When they hit one of our panzers there is so often a deep long explosion, a roar as the fuel burns, a roar too loud, thank God, to let us hear the cries of the crew . . .'

Rarely has the importance of technical superiority been so clearly demonstrated. Track widths, ground clearance, power-to-weight ratio, the angle of sloped armour . . these statistics, allied with courage and determination, could balance the sophisticated training and cavalry elan of the panzers. They formed an equation to which the solution was charred flesh, broken bodies, and blood.

The Russian command was in no doubt about the importance of Katukov's battle in showing that the panzers could be beaten. He was immediately promoted major-general, awarded the Order of Lenin, while the survivors of 4th Tank Brigade received the honour of being renamed 1st Guards Tank Brigade – the first tank unit to be given the 'Guards' designation.

Actions like Katukov's were vitally important if the Russian armour was to delay the German offensive long enough for the combination of the Russian winter and a Russian counter-attack to give it the coup de grace. Similar groups of T-34s, small in numbers but terrifying in effectiveness, hung like wolves on the flanks of the panzer divisions, striking down from the hills on their broad tracks, inflicting casualties, and disappearing again into the twilight which, every day, was becoming longer and longer.

The panzer divisions themselves were making superhuman efforts to reach Moscow, but only prodigies of staff work were edging them forward.

Above: German infantry in snow-suits examine KV-1 heavy tank knocked out on the Leningrad front. *Below:* German heavy artillery on the Donetz

Above: Leading a counterattack: a T-34 plunges into the smoke of battle. *Below:*
The anti-tank role: a T-34 engages light German armour

At first, the enemy was mud. As Second Panzer Army moved forward again near Tula, its tanks and lorries were gradually left behind, helplessly embedded in the liquid glue of the roads. The advance of this armoured army was now maintained almost entirely by the infantry divisions, with the divisional staff officers, in a strange echo of 1918, travelling on horseback. Oats were easier to find than petrol on the Tula road.

Only when the winter began to bite hard, and the frosts hardened the ground, did the German armour once more move forward. Tank warfare in these conditions was like nothing the Germans had ever known. General Gunther Blumentritt, who at this time was chief of staff to Kluge's army in front of Moscow, wrote later:

'. . . For a few hours each day there was limited visibility at the front. Until nine o'clock in the morning the wintry landscape was shrouded in a thick fog. Gradually a red ball, the sun, became visible in the eastern sky, and by about eleven it was possible to see a little. At three o'clock dusk set in and an hour later it was almost completely dark . . .'

In the tanks the gun lubricant froze, and so did the mechanism of the guns. It was bitterly cold in the turrets, and at night the engines had to be run for fifteen minutes every four hours to stop them being burst by the frost. No glycerine was available for anti-freeze, and, as an added measure, small fires were lit beneath the tank hulls at night to help keep the engines warm. The inside of a peasant hut seemed like paradise to German soldiers.

Yet Russian armour was not afraid to try to operate during the icy nights which paralysed the panzers. Curiously, for tank crews whose training at this stage must have been rudimentary, Soviet armoured doctrine from

Troops of the Waffen-SS in snow uniforms: December 1942

the first taught the value of night attacks. Such attacks by armour are one of the most difficult operations of war, yet for infantry who have to face them they can be a terrifying experience. Such an attack proved to be so for a battalion of the 258th Infantry Division on 2nd December.

On this day, according to a military legend of doubtful authenticity, the advance troops of this division had actually glimpsed, as daylight faded in the short afternoon, the glinting of the setting sun on the onion-towers of the Kremlin. What is certain, however, is that Russian staff officers plotting their position on the headquarters battle maps must have thought them to be dangerously near. They were in the village of Yushkovo, exactly twenty-seven miles from Moscow, but they were in poor shape. Their mobile support was tenuous, consisting of three self-propelled guns and a single 88mm anti-aircraft gun.

During the morning, thirty men of the battalion had reported frost-bitten feet of varying severity, but there was no transport to get them to a dressing station. As the appalling cold of the night drew on, the battalion crowded into the handful of straw-roofed peasant houses that still stood, wedged round the stoves with the surly Russian peasants, while the sentries took hot bricks from the stoves every hour to lay on the breeches of their freezing Spandau machine-guns.

Into this scene of military misery, two hours before midnight, rumbled a group of T-34s. The tank machine-guns, firing tracer, set ablaze the roofs of every hut: the periodic crash of the 76.2mm tank cannons punctuated the screams and shouts of Germans tumbling out into the numbing cold.

Sticking to their gun, the crew of the 88mm destroyed two T-34s as they waddled down the burning street of Yushkovo. A moment later the gun crew died beside their smashed weapon as another Russian tank

Above: A drink from the brook: Russian prisoners, July 1942. *Below:* German flame-thrower

Above: German infantry pass a KV-1 with track hanging loose, May 1942.
Below: Death in the snow: Russian reconnaissance patrol caught by German fire,

picked them off. Two of the three German self-propelled guns were now ablaze, but a determined German lieutenant attacked the T-34s with mines – an attack to which they were especially vulnerable in the darkness. All night long, as the fighting moved among the blazing huts, the German infantry lay and froze in the allotments and gardens of Yushkovo. When morning came, the T-34s withdrew. They had lost heavily themselves. Six of them were burning in the main street, but they had destroyed the 88mm gun, and two of the self-propelled guns, and had killed many German infantrymen. Seventy seriously wounded men lay in the piercing cold of the potato cellars, and the battalion was no longer a viable force. Moscow, for 258th Infantry Division, was out of the question. In another small but significant action, Russian armour had imposed an unacceptable delay on the German command. The German armies were now stretched beyond their safety level. In Second Panzer Army, Guderian was discovering bitterly that open flanks when standing still are a very different thing from open flanks when in full victory cry across a prostrate countryside. He wrote to his wife:

'... The icy cold, the wretched accommodation, the shortage of clothing, the heavy losses of men and equipment, the wretched state of our fuel supplies, all this makes the duties of a commander a misery, and the longer it goes on the more I am crushed by the enormous responsibility I bear ...'

The moment had come for the Russian counter-attack, and the man who was eager to deliver it was already in command. Stalin had chosen Marshal Georgi Zhukov for the crucial Western Front covering Moscow.

Hard, restless, furiously energetic,

Panzer leader: Guderian with his tank troops, September 1941

Zhukov burst into his command like a demon in a fairy tale. He had learned his fighting technique on the Manchurian border against the Japanese in 1938. Briefly, it was to allow the enemy to expend himself, with the maximum possible casualties, while he himself cautiously amassed superior *local* forces behind the battle. Then, when the enemy was stretched to his limit, Zhukov would counter-attack into the disorganised and disheartened areas of a failed enemy attack. These were the tactics practised by Montgomery, on a smaller scale, at Alam Halfa and Alamein. They were perfect tactics against the German panzers, and they suited the limited training of the Russian tank crews, because they meant that Zhukov would have to keep a very tight hand on his armour. They sound simple enough, perhaps, but they required enormous reservoirs of courage from the shock-absorbing Russian infantry, and a desperately-learned skill from the scanty Russian tank units. Zhukov knew that tanks would be vital for his planned counter-attack, and under his urging *Stavka* now withdrew from the Far East the eight remaining intact tank brigades of the Red Army, fifteen rifle divisions, and three cavalry. The Russian command was prepared to risk a Japanese attack in order to defeat the German drive on Moscow.

Exactly four days after the T-34s had set ablaze the German billets in the village of Yushkovo, Zhukov launched his counter-offensive. He had scraped together what he could find, including some of the excellent Siberian infantry from the Far East, but his tank support was not nearly as great as he needed. His total forces amounted to seventeen armies (a Russian army was usually about equal to a British or American army corps), though the term 'army' was perhaps a somewhat ambitious one for some of the scratch formations which had now been thrown together. One of these 'armies' was a tank force

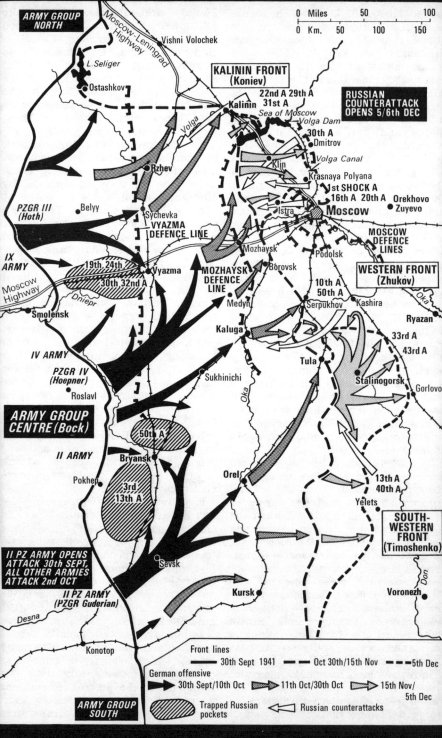

The Battlefront: December 1941 - April 1942

commanded by the excellent Katukov who had given Langermann such a bloody nose near Tula a couple of months before. This formation consisted largely of the precious T-34s which had survived the winter battles, stiffened, perhaps, with some of the tanks and crews from the Far East. It was to these tanks, more than to any other part of the Russian armies, that Zhukov now gave an order which showed how clearly he understood the role of his scanty armour in the counter-blow. His special directive ordered, unequivocally:

'Pursuit must be at a high speed and the enemy not allowed to break contact. Widespread use must be made of strong leading detachments for seizure of road junctions and bottlenecks, and for disorganizing enemy march and combat formations. 'I categorically forbid frontal attacks against enemy fortified points. Forward echelons should by-pass these without delay, and leave them to be destroyed by following echelons . . .'

This was an echo of the doctrine of the 'expanding torrent' of armour put forward in Britain by Liddell Hart in the 1930s, and adopted by Guderian and other panzer leaders in the campaign in France in 1940. Above all, they were tactics made for the T-34, with its long operating range, and formidable automotive performance and hitting power. Both the tank and the tactics would have delighted Tukhachevsky.

Zhukov's battle was a limited success in a purely military sense, but it was completely decisive in relieving Moscow. The threat of the German Army Group Centre was hurled back, approaching in some areas the point of disintegration. At no major point however was Zhukov - in spite of the insistent urging of Stalin and *Stavka* - able to take advantage of this to turn in on the flanks and envelop the greater portion of the German army. Leaving hundreds of tanks and guns behind in the drifting snow, the Germans fell back from Moscow, while Zhukov advanced his Western Front between fo rty-five and sixty-five miles. This, he recorded drily, 'somewhat improved the operational strategic situation in the west . . .' He was too good a soldier not to know that Stalin's repeated call for a great Cannae-like victory of envelopment was, as yet, merely a dream - though thousands of Russians had to die unnecessarily in the snows of January and February before *Stavka* grudgingly acknowledged that it could not be realised. The reason was simple. Zhukov did not have enough tanks for such an operation, even if he had - which he did not - enough trained crews.

'Tankov niet,' Stalin had told him when he asked for more armour at the start of the offensive. 'No tanks . . . we don't have any . . .' That was the end of any Russian hope of a decisive destruction of the German armies conducting Operation *Barbarossa*. Zhukov himself summed it up succinctly:

'The Soviet counter-offensive . . . was conducted under the difficult conditions of a snowy, cold winter . . . without numerical superiority . . . Our mechanised and tank formations were below strength, and we know from experience that under such conditions, offensive operations cannot be carried out on a large scale. The enemy's manoeuvres can be anticipated, his forces outflanked, and his escape routes cut only with powerful mechanised and tank units . . .'

However, the first half of the Russian equation of victory had been achieved. Zhukov's Moscow counter-blow was giving the Russians time to learn. This applied most of all to the armour. Mistakes, wrong assumptions, over-confidence, even disaster lay ahead. But the Russian tank forces had the equipment, and, in the end, enough time. They also had, at last, a commander who had a very clear idea of what tanks could and could not do.

Challenge and response

Not surprisingly, the difficulties which the German panzer forces encountered because of the very nature of the geographical and climatic conditions of the campaign in Russia increased their anxieties about Russian technical superiority. The T-34, in fact, assumed a bogeyman character for the German army, in spite both of the comparatively unsophisticated way in which it was handled by the Russian command in the early days and of the very heavy losses which the Germans succeeded in inflicting on Russian armour.

Guderian, who was no longer the impatient saddle-general of 1940, called for a commission of representatives of the army ordnance office, the armaments ministry, the tank designers and tank manufacturers to come immediately to the front to examine knocked-out and captured T-34s. He also requested the rapid production of a standard anti-tank gun able to destroy the new Russian tanks.

German tank design and production were now thrown into a state of near-panic. The hurried re-equipment of the Mark III with the 50mm L60 gun could be regarded as no more than a stop-gap, in view of the poor comparison this tank made with the T-34 in other important respects. In a hasty search for a tank which would be more nearly equal to the Russian armoured menace, the immediate choice, by necessity, fell upon the Mark IV. This tank now began to have its low-velocity 75mm gun replaced by a longer version which gave more than double the muzzle velocity. The Mark IV, in fact, became the mainstay of the German armoured forces for the rest of the war, accepting better versions of the 75mm gun as time went on. In its later models, this tank was nearly the equal of the T-34/76.

To be equal, however, was hardly enough. Experiments had already

Russian tank commander waits with a flare pistol to give the signal to advance

Above: German Mark IV with track plates welded as extra protection on turret top.
Below: The 45-ton Panther: teething troubles ahead

been conducted with a new 56-ton tank, the Mark VI, which carried an 88mm gun and had a thickness of 100mm of armour on the front of its turret, making it invulnerable except at very close range to the T-34's 76.2mm gun. The prototype of this monster was rushed forward to get it ready for Hitler's birthday on 20th April 1942, and it went into production three months later. It received the most charismatic name of all German tanks: the Tiger.

The use of the Tiger in German panzer divisions was a signal that the uncompromisingly offensive spirit of the panzers was beginning to be eroded by events. The Tiger was an admirable defensive weapon, used either as an assault tank supporting infantry, or as a static strongpoint. In terms of mobility, it was eclipsed by the Russian tanks: its speed across country was about twelve miles per hour, its range was less than sixty-five miles, and its power-to-weight ratio was a dismal 12.3 horse-power per ton. This last performance figure represented a grave handicap when Tigers were needed as mobile forces. German panzer generals, who sometimes regarded them as a mixed blessing, found that they were prone to breakdown, and that every broken-down Tiger needed another Tiger to tow it away.

The panzer forces, indeed, required another tank – something nearer in style to the T-34, but better protected and more powerfully armed. From the front in Russia came the suggestion – a galling one, no doubt, to German designers – that the T-34 should for the moment simply be accurately copied in a German version. This proposal was immediately rejected, less for reasons of pride than because the Russian aluminium engine could not easily be mass produced by available German plant.

Instead, work began on a new design, the Mark V, later called the Panther. This was a 45-ton tank which, like the T-34, had sloped and angled armour.

It was equipped with an even higher velocity gun, the long L70 version of the 75mm. The turret armour reached 120mm, yet the Panther had a road speed of twenty-eight miles per hour and a power-weight ratio of more than 15 horse-power to the ton. It might be thought that the Germans had at last found the answer to the T-34. So, up to a point, they had, for the Panther was probably the most impressive tank design produced during the Second World War. It began to be delivered to German units in the spring of 1943, but, as we shall see, it had serious teething troubles ahead of it. Meanwhile, the Russians were not standing still.

From the start of the *Barbarossa* campaign, Russian designers had been strongly aware that they had a winner in the T-34, but that the early models had deficiencies which must be corrected. Not a great deal could be done in the turmoil and confusion of moving the tank factories east to the Urals in the early months of the war, though some temporary improvements were carried out where these would not interfere with desperately-needed production. A new cast turret was provided for later models; the vulnerable overhang between it and the hull was considerably reduced; the fuel supply was increased; and the gearbox improved. Extra armour was welded on to some models, while on the new turrets the thickness now reached 90mm. During 1942, the Russian factories produced more than 5,000 of the 76mm gun T-34s, but it was now clear that more far-reaching changes must be made if the tank was to keep pace with the new generation of German machines.

The disadvantages of the two-man turret had long made themselves felt, and a radical change was now ordered. The existing T-34 chassis was adapted to take a cast, three-man turret, and a much more powerful gun. This was the long 85mm which, like the German 88mm, was adapted from a pre-war anti-aircraft gun. Its performance

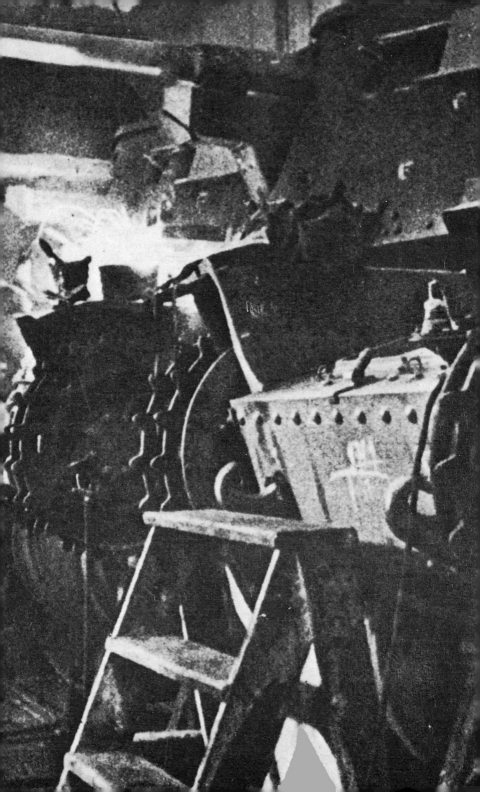

Left: Production line in a German factory. *Above:* A Russian factory: down comes a turret for a T-34

was roughly similar to that of the 88mm fitted in the early versions of the German Tiger: the 85mm fired a 21.5 lb shot at a muzzle velocity of 2,600 feet per second, compared with the 88mm gun's 22.25 lb shot at 2,657 feet per second. The Panther's 75mm fired a much smaller shot – 15 lbs – but the muzzle velocity was much higher at 3,068 feet per second.

For the T-34, of course, heavier armour, a heavier gun and a heavier turret inevitably meant a heavier tank, and a consequent decrease in operational flexibility. Neverthless, the vital statistics of the T-34/85 are a tribute to the efficiency of the amended design. The overall weight of the tank rose from 27 to 32 tons, and its effective range fell from 280 miles to about 190. Its speed was a little below thirty miles per hour – about the same as the Panther. When it

went into production in the winter of 1943, the T-34/85 could be considered to be more formidable than any tank in production in any Allied army, though perhaps a little less so than the Panther. This last point would not have been yielded by the Russians themselves. Reports from the front showed that Russian tank crews preferred the T-34/85 when they compared it with captured Panthers – possibly because the T-34 retained a great deal of its former excellent automotive performance, while the early Panthers suffered from various troubles, including an alarming tendency to catch fire very easily.

Perhaps the most considerable advantage of the T-34/85 was that it offered an acceptable counter-weight to the new generation of German tanks without materially affecting the speed and volume of Russian tank production. Koshkin was now in his grave, but the excellence and adaptability of his basic design gave the Russian factories an enormous advan-

tage when it came to turning out sheer numbers.

During 1943, Soviet tank production reached 10,000 machines, of which approximately 6,000 were T-34/76 models, with possibly only a few hundred of the new T-34/85s coming off the production lines at the end of the year. In spite of a certain amount of re-tooling necessary for the new model, Russian tank production again rose during 1944 to almost 12,000 machines, of which, again, about 65 per cent were T-34/85s.

The German story was different. About 1,780 Panthers were produced in 1943, and 3,740 in 1944, while about 1,350 Tigers were produced between August 1942 and August 1944. In fact,

Left: The answer to the Panther : the T-34/85 in night action on the First Byelorussian Front 1945. *Below* T-34/85s move into action on the Southern Front

the backbone of the German armoured forces remained the various up-gunned versions of the Mark IV, to which the T-34/85 was distinctly superior. More than 9,000 Mark IVs were produced during the war – nearly 3,400 of them in 1944. Thus, while the Panther might be considered to be marginally a better machine than the T-34/85, the overall superiority in design remained with Russia, simply because it proved impossible for the German armaments industry to switch production sufficiently for the new German designs to outnumber the T-34s.

This was not, at first, fully grasped in Germany in the flury of self-congratulation which accompanied the production of the early models of the Tiger and the Panther. It is an interesting reflection that the T-34 *almost* achieved the annihilation of the German panzer forces without firing a further shot. Seduced by visions of

regaining technical mastery, early in 1943 the OKH requested that all tank production programmes except for the Tiger and Panther should be abandoned in order to concentrate production on these two.

'This new plan,' Guderian commented sardonically, 'contained only one major weakness: with the abandonment of the Mark IV, Germany would until further notice be limited to the production of twenty-five Tigers a month. This would certainly have led to the defeat of the German army in the very near future . . . the Russians would have won the war even without the help of their Western allies . . . no power on earth could have stopped them . . .'

Left: A celebrated name : the Tiger I
Below: German troops surrender to a Russian tank unit near Kharkov 1942

However, into this mounting German crisis now stepped the figure of Guderian himself, recalled to command by Hitler as Inspector General of Armoured Troops, with what was virtually a free hand in training and organising the panzer forces. For commanders like Zhukov, wielding the T-34s and KVs as the edge of the Russian sword, Guderian's appointment would mean new problems, not least because the whole nature of armoured warfare was changing. Under Guderian's careful guiding hand, both the quality and the quantity of the panzer forces began once more to be built up. Yet the changes in armoured warfare, it would soon be seen, suited the temperament of the Russian commanders better than that of the panzer generals, and also suited the nature of the tactics which the very limitations of Soviet training imposed.

Learning the lesson

The possession of armoured forces seems to have a compulsive effect upon dictators, perhaps because a tank army offers – superficially, at least – an instrument for the instant imposition of the dictator's will. At any rate, as the Russian winter softened into spring, it was the turn of Stalin to make for himself the mistake that Hitler had made in the previous summer – under-estimation of the enemy, and over-estimation of the capabilities of his own armoured force.

Russian armoured organisation as the new campaigning season opened was still based on the independent tank brigade, of which the tank content was usually about fifty machines – a mixture of T-34s and KV-1s. These brigades grew rapidly in number during 1942: there were about twenty available at the beginning of May, but the Germans claimed to have identified 138 by the end of the year. However, it was quicker, easier, and cheaper to manufacture a T-34 than to choose and train its crew. The difficulties of swiftly acquiring a proper reservoir of trained tank crews for the new brigades meant that their use would be strictly limited – and would often be confined purely to infantry support. A panzer division is not produced overnight: the whole command structure of the Russian armour, from the corps commander down to the over-worked men in the T-34 turret, needed to be revised and refined if it was to be used properly. The brigade was too small a formation for use in a hammer blow, and yet the Russian command was not yet experienced enough to handle armour, offensively, in larger masses. Zhukov knew this, but Stalin did not.

Stalin now intended to assuage his frustrations of the previous year by offensive operations on a grand scale. The State Defence Committee met at the end of March, and a lively dispute

German armoured column advances across the Steppe towards Stalingrad

Marshal Bagramyan

Marshal Shaposhnikov

Marshal Vasilevsky

Marshal Stalin

ensued among Russia's military leaders. Zhukov had already expressed his views: he wanted to launch a limited offensive to eliminate the dangerous German salient which threatened Moscow in the Rzhev-Vyasma area. However, Stalin and part of the Russian general staff were interested in operations farther south. Stalin aimed at nothing less than a great stroke to recapture Kharkov. This would require the bulk of the T-34s and KV-1s of the painfully-reconstituted Russian armoured force.

The State Defence Committee on this occasion was attended by Voroshilov, Timoshenko, Shaposhnikov (the Russian chief of Staff), Vasilevsky, Bagrammyan, Zhukov – and, of course, Stalin. Of those present Shaposhnikov was nearest to Zhukov's attitude with regard to new offensives. He, too, wanted active defence until Russia was stronger. Stalin, in a flash strangely reminiscent of Churchill, turned on them all 'We cannot remain on the defensive and sit on our hands until the Germans strike first. We must launch preventive strikes . . .'

This was also the thinking of Timoshenko, who was now to command the South West zone of operations. He announced that his troops were ready for an offensive, and that such an offensive should be undertaken as a preventive measure, to disrupt German plans for an attack of their own. Shaposhnikov, no doubt feeling Stalin's speculative eye upon him, remained silent at this vital moment, and the die was cast.

In April, Timoshenko received his orders. He was to attack the Germans in the area of Kharkov, and recapture the city. Timoshenko himself now had the bit between his teeth, and he was eager to expand this not inconsiderable operation into one of even wider scope, aimed at driving the Germans back to the Dniepr river. He believed that the most effective blow he could strike would be to launch his armour into the German concentrations preparing for their own offensive. For this purpose, he had under his command fourteen of the twenty tank brigades now available.

Rigid and clumsy though it was, Timoshenko's attack at first succeeded under its sheer impetus. He broke into the positions of Paulus's Sixth Army for depths which varied between fourteen and twenty miles. Nemesis was waiting, however, in the shape of Kleist's First Panzer Army, which had been concentrating, ready for a German offensive, at Kramatorsk in the base of the salient which Timoshenko was attacking. This concentration was out of reach of Timoshenko's initial attack, and was thus in effect a most formidable mobile armoured reserve, whose tanks were fuelled up, full of ammunition, and ready to move. Timoshenko seemed resolutely to turn his eyes away from this threat, although, according to Zhukov, even Stalin was concerned about it. Timoshenko told Stalin, in effect, that Kleist at Kramatorsk was something of a paper tiger. His views were supported by General Nikita Kruschev, who at this time was Timoshenko's political commissar. Within a few days, Kleist's well-trained tank crews proved them wrong.

On 17th May, Kleist struck. His forces comprised two panzer divisions, one panzergrenadier division, and eight infantry divisions. From a military point of view, the situation was grotesque. As part of Timoshenko's forces – Gorodniansky's Sixth Army and Kharitonov's Ninth – swung north towards Kharkov, Kleist's tanks hit the long extended flank. Meanwhile, following its orders, the Russian armour was actually pressing on out of the main battle area. All was rapidly confusion, especially in the Ninth Army, which was encircled and destroyed piecemeal. There were no adequate Russian reserves, and Timoshenko, with his armour strung out and in disarray, could do nothing to put the situation right.

Above: Summer on the Steppe: Russian infantry and T-34s assemble for an attack.
Below: Mopping up: Russian tanks flush out a German platoon

On 18th May, his staff telephoned *Stavka* asking if he could break off the battle, but received a dusty answer from Stalin. He was told to go on attacking 'to the end.' It was another day before *Stavka* gave qualified permission to go on the defensive, but by then the damage had been done. Encircled and chopped up one by one, the Russian armies were comprehensively defeated. Two army commanders were dead – Gorodniansky of Sixth Army and Podlas of Ninth. More than 250,000 Russians were captured, and – just as important – the fourteen precious tank brigades were largely destroyed. Zhukov later summed it up: 'When we analyse the failure, it is easy to see that the basic reason for it was an under-estimation of the serious threat posed to the South West command, and our failure to position Supreme Headquarters reserves in the area. If several reserve armies had been available in the rear of the front, we could have avoided the catastrophe of the Kharkov offensive...'

The Kharkov debacle left a savage scar upon Russian confidence. Twenty-four years later, Kruschev's own account of how Stalin had acted 'contrary to common sense' formed a notable part of his celebrated report to the 20th Congress, in which he sought to puncture the myth of Stalin's infallibility. However, in 1942 one clear military deduction could be drawn from the whole sorry, bloody business: the Russian armour, though building up in numbers, still had a very, very great deal to learn. For the failure was not wholly at the level of Timoshenko. Much lower down the scale, essential qualities were still lacking. There were still not enough Katukovs. German opinion of the lower and middle levels of command in Russian armoured formations was that they were poor in the summer of 1942, that they lacked the ability to make quick decisions and had little tactical insight even at battalion or company level, and that the cavalry daring of the German panzers simply was not there.

One panzer staff officer wrote: 'In tight masses they groped around in the main German battle zone; they moved hesitantly and without any plan. They got in each other's way, they blundered against our anti-tank guns, or, after penetrating our front they did nothing to exploit their advantage and stood inactive and idle. Those were the days when isolated German anti-tank guns or 88s had their heyday, and sometimes one gun would shoot up and knock out more than thirty tanks an hour. We thought that the Russians had created a tool which they would never be able to handle expertly, but even in the winter of 1942-3 there were signs of improvement...' Katukov, outside Tula, had already shown what could be done with intelligence, determination – and T-34s. But before that kind of action could be repeated on a larger scale, the Russian tanks had to face a summer of struggle and loss.

After the Kharkov disaster, the Russian crisis was graver even than that of the previous winter in front of Moscow. The campaigning season was now open for the panzers, and the Russian tanks were too low, both in numbers and command quality, to resist them. Through the gap torn in the Kharkov front poured Kleist's First Panzer Army, roaming virtually at will. Within a few weeks, it was down among the western oilfields of the Caucasus, at Maikop. An even greater threat was posed by Hoth's Fourth Panzer Army, which had been ordered to strike through the gap between Kharkov and Kursk, reach the Don river at Voronezh, and then turn south towards Rostov. Within ten days, Hoth's tanks had raced 120 miles across the steppe, signalling their coming with the huge brown pall of dust thrown up by the tank tracks.

At Goroditny, halfway between Kursk and Voronezh, Hoth met a desperate counter-attack by Russia tanks. The Russian tactics were

Above: German Wasp 10.5cm self propelled guns. *Below:* German mortar team outside Sebastopol 1942. Note the man carrying mortar base plate

Above: Moving east: German Mark IIIs on the march. *Below:* Temporary armour: a Mark III with track plates welded for extra protection

clumsy, and the T-34s hit the German anti-tank guns head-on, and were then taken in the rear and flank by German armour. Brushing aside the remnants of the Russian force, Hoth entered Voronezh on 3rd July.

However, at this crucial moment, Hitler committed a fatal strategic error. Not for the first or the last time in his life, he was mesmerised by the dazzling success of the technique of the *blitzkrieg* into thinking that speed and mobility were the only important elements in war. Impatient to get Kleist into the Caucasus, he decided to divert Hoth temporarily to help support First Panzer Army across the Don. In the event, Hoth was more of a hindrance than a help to Kleist, since Russian resistance was both light and confused, and the milling about of two German panzer armies at the river crossings actually held up the progress of First Panzer Army. On 29th July, Hoth received new orders. He was to swing up to take Stalingrad, which was now the objective of Paulus's Sixth Army, from the south-west. Hoth had originally been spearheading Paulus in the drive on the city, and his withdrawal to help Kleist had left Paulus without the armoured tip to his advance. Now Hitler's new order came too late. Paulus's Sixth Army, still moving on Hoth's original route, was moving too slowly without its panzers. Both Paulus and Hoth arrived at Stalingrad too late. Kleist's own view of Hitler's error was expressed after the war: 'The Fourth Panzer Army was advancing on my left. It could have taken Stalingrad without a fight at the end of July, but

The feared adversary, a German 8.8cm gun in the anti-tank role, with a claimed kill at left

Left: Stalingrad : German motorised troops. *Above:* On the skyline : German supplies move up. *Below:* German artillerymen observe fire with a periscope

was diverted south to help me in crossing the Don. I did not need its aid, and it merely congested the roads I was using. When it turned north again, a fortnight later, the Russians had gathered just sufficient forces at Stalingrad to check it . . .'

The capture and destruction at Stalingrad of the German Sixth Army are not the province of this account, and have been fully described elsewhere in this series. (*Stalingrad*, by Geoffrey Jukes – Battle Book 3.) Yet for Russian armour, they were of vital importance, because they meant two things. First, the *blitzkrieg*, as practised by Hoth and Kleist in the vast Russian steppe, had been proved – though narrowly – to produce success but not victory. Second, the panzer mood was in any case changing under the influence of the frustration and eventual catastrophe on the Volga. The Russian Marshal Chuikov, who won his fame as the defender of Stalingrad, noted during the summer of 1942:

'I was expecting close combined operations between the enemy's artillery and ground forces, a precise organisation of the artillery barrage, a lightning-fast manoeuvre of shell and wheel. But this was not the case. I encountered the far from new method of slow wearing-down, trench by trench . . . The German tanks did not go into action without infantry and air support. On the battlefield there was no evidence of the prowess of German tank crews, their courage and speed in action, about which foreign newspapers had written. The reverse was true, in fact: they operated sluggishly, extremely cautiously, and indecisively . . .'

After Stalingrad, armoured warfare changed, and both sides were feeling their way towards new techniques and tactics. For the Germans, the day of the *blitzkrieg* was over. Kleist's

The panzer veteran: Colonel-General Hermann Hoth with Rumanian General Dragalina

rush into the Caucasus with First Panzer Army was the last of its kind. It had been less successful, in any case, than it had seemed to be at first sight. Kleist had been held up beyond Maikop by sheer lack of petrol, and then, after the destruction of Paulus at Stalingrad, almost fatally threatened by Russian armies striking down the valley of the Don behind his left flank. Only a last minute withdrawal through Rostov had saved him. '*Kaukasus, hin und zuruck*' – the Caucasus round-trip – was how German soldiers sardonically described this operation.

The Russians had never fully identified themselves with *blitzkrieg* tactics at any time, simply because they had not had time to learn them. Timoshenko's somewhat amateurish efforts in this regard had been an unqualified disaster. Probably at no level in command were the Russians, at this stage in the war, capable of operating armoured divisions as Guderian and Hoth had done in France and in the opening days of *Barbarossa*. Thus the Russians, at any rate, did not have the disadvantage of having to learn the changes in mood, tactics and weapons which now faced the panzer crews.

Above all, it was weapons which were changing the nature of armoured war. The new heavy tanks – the Tiger and the Stalin (of which more will be said later) were a world away from the Mark III and the T-34. A more far-reaching change even than these, however, was now being made in the armoured forces of both sides. This change implicity recognised that the tank was now a vulnerable mobile gun rather than an invincible armoured horse. A new kind of armoured weapon was created, the self-propelled gun built on the chassis of tanks like the T-34 and the Mark III. It was a weapon which suited Zhukov more than Guderian, and which was better adapted to the growing Russian skills than to the flagging elan of the panzer divisions.

The mobile gun

The armoured self-propelled guns which began to enter service on an increasing scale on both sides of the Eastern Front in 1942 could trace their origin back to German ideas before 1939. As early as 1936, German designers were asked to produce a close-support gun on a mobile self-propelled chassis for infantry support as well as an anti-tank role. Early versions of this were mounted on the chassis of the Mark III, and carried the short, low-velocity 75mm gun. The anti-tank role of such machines became sharply more important after the Germans encountered the T-34 in battle during 1941, and on 22nd December of that year orders were given that an effective armoured tank destroyer, capable of meeting the T-34 – at least with regard to gun power – on something like even terms, must be produced immediately while work went on apace on a more effective weapon.

The chassis for this vehicle was that of the excellent Czech 38 tank – and the gun was a tribute to the Russians. In fact, this vehicle, known in the German army as the Marder III, was equipped with captured Russian 76.2mm guns of the type used in the T-34. The Marder IIIs, of which about 120 had been produced by the spring of 1942, were theoretically the only German armour capable of tackling the T-34 at that time. They were followed by various, progressively better-armed models based upon the Mark IV, Panther, and Tiger chassis.

Thus the self-propelled gun evolved from the early *sturmgeschutz* or assault gun meant to provide close support for the infantry to the sophisticated *panzerjager* (tank hunter) or *jagdpanzer* (tank destroyer) of the later years of the war. Such a weapon offered both advantages and disadvantages when compared with the tank proper. Its most serious handicap was that

East Prussia, 1945: Stalin II tanks advance

Above: The Stalin I. *Below:* Stalin III: the last of a wartime line

it possessed no turret in the conventional sense, but merely a fighting compartment – sometimes open at the top and thus vulnerable to airburst shells – in which the gun either could not be traversed at all, or could be moved only a few degrees left or right. Thus the whole vehicle had to be moved on its tracks in order to lay the gun – with the consequent disadvantages of slow gun-laying, and of revealing the gun's position to the enemy.

Against this, however, there were very considerable compensations. The lack of a moving turret simplified production, and brought down the cost. From the crew's point of view, the larger fighting compartment meant a consequent ease of loading and a more rapid rate of fire. It also meant that the *jagdpanzer* could take a gun at least one size up from that fitted in the tank version on the same chassis. For instance, the *jagdpanzer* on the Mark III chassis was equipped with a long 75mm gun, though the tank version still had the 50mm. There was one further advantage: the *jagdpanzer* necessarily had a lower silhouette than the tank, and this could be a decisive factor when trying to use the limited ground cover sometimes available on the rolling Russian steppe.

For the Germans, the *jagdpanzer* symbolised the change which had come over their thinking about the panzers. It was essentially, in its anti-tank role, a defensive weapon, used best in ambush or in semi-fixed positions. Hitler had already confided to some of his generals that 'the day of the tank may soon be over.' This pessimism was prompted in part by the development of hollow-charge, bazooka-type weapons which could be carried by individual infantry men and were capable, when used with courage and determination, of knocking out a heavy tank.

However, when the Russians enthusiastically adopted the *jagdpanzer* idea, it was in a somewhat different spirit.

The use of a heavily-armed but comparatively primitive 'tank' in some of their close-knit formations suited them very well: the easing of production problems meant that the sheer armoured mass at which they were aiming would be achieved more easily. It was simpler and quicker to train gunners and fighting crews for a self-propelled gun than for a tank, and in any case, the whole of the Russian artillery tradition was built round the conception of direct fire support. Russian designers had, in fact, flirted with the idea of self-propelled guns early in the 1930s, though they had never put a model into production.

During 1942, however, the growing need for effective, quickly-produced armour resulted in the design and manufacture of the first of the Russian self-propelled guns, the Samokyana Ustanokova 76. This was the tried and proven 76.2mm gun mounted on a modification of the T-70 light tank chassis. It was an open-topped machine with a higher silhouette than was desirable, and in any case by the time it came into general service at the end of 1942 its 76.2mm gun was inadequate against the new Tigers – and soon the Panthers – which the Germans were beginning to employ. Thus the SU-76 was being rapidly overtaken by events, and immediate orders were placed for a heavier model.

The basis for the new machine was the chassis of the T-34/76, but the gun was the 85mm which was now being fitted into the next generation of T-34 tanks. The SU-85 was designed in a tank-destroying role, but its gun – like the earlier 76.2mm – was, of course, also highly effective with high-explosive shells, and could thus easily adopt the *sturmgeschutz* role of infantry support. The speed-up in production of the SU models compared with that of the tanks meant that the SU-85 came into service at roughly the same time as the T-34/85. Another model, the SU-100, also on the T-34 chassis but armed with a 100mm gun,

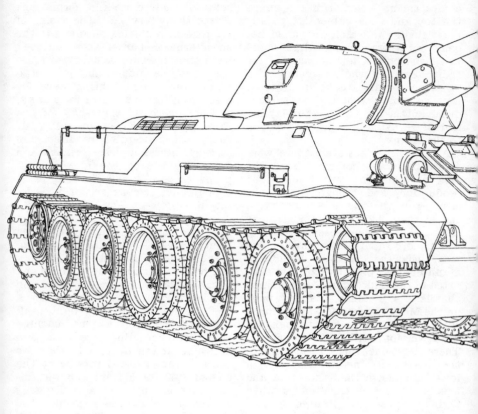

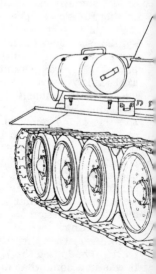

Su85 based on T34 chassis. *Crew:* 4.
Combat weight: 30 tons. *Armament:*
88mm gun. *Length:* 19 feet 6 inches.
Width: 9 feet 10 inches. *Height:* 7 feet
9 inches. *Engine:* 500 hp. *Speed:* 32mph

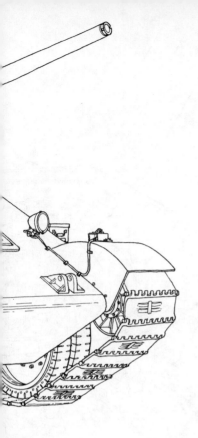

Russian Cruiser Tank T34/76. *Weight:* 27 tons 16 cwts fully stowed – less crew. *Crew:* 4 men. *Armament:* one 76.2mm gun model F.34 and one 7.62mm DT machine gun in coaxial turret mount, one 7.62mm DT machine gun in armoured ball mount on off-side of front glacis plate. *Rounds carried:* 76.2mm 77 rounds, 7.62mm 2898–3906 rounds MG ammunition – tanks without radio carry 4725 rounds. *Length with gun at 12o/c:* 21 feet 7 inches. *Width:* 9 feet 10 inches. *Height:* 7 feet 9 inches. *Engine:* 500 hp diesel V-12 model V-2. *Speed:* 53.5 kph 33 mph. *Armour thickness:* maximum 65mm – minimum 15mm

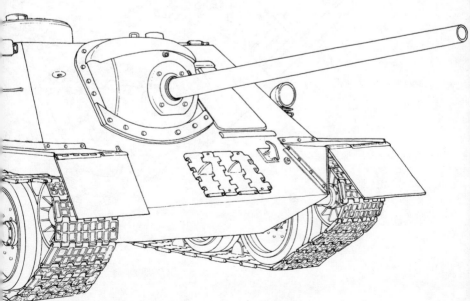

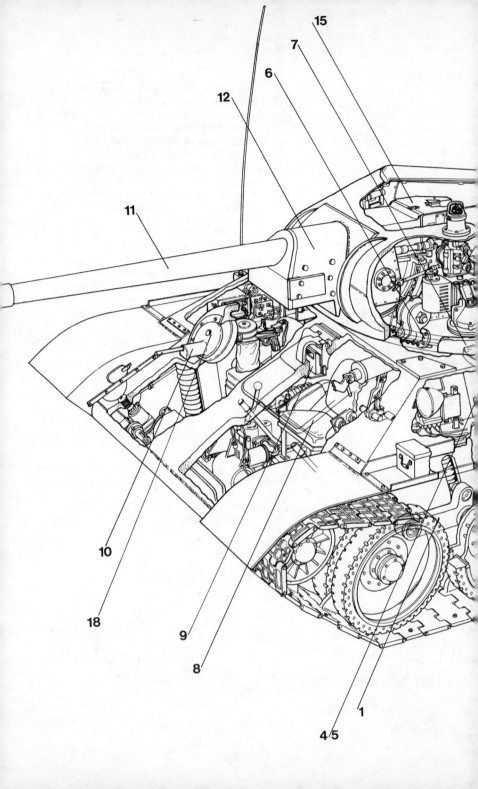

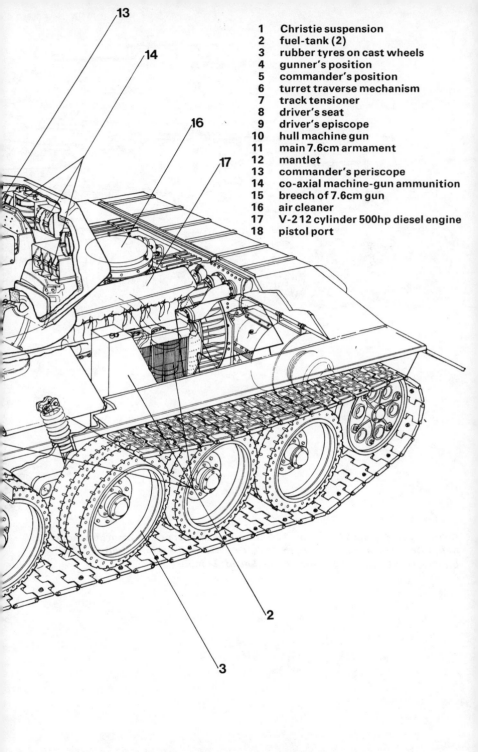

1   Christie suspension
2   fuel-tank (2)
3   rubber tyres on cast wheels
4   gunner's position
5   commander's position
6   turret traverse mechanism
7   track tensioner
8   driver's seat
9   driver's episcope
10 hull machine gun
11 main 7.6cm armament
12 mantlet
13 commander's periscope
14 co-axial machine-gun ammunition
15 breech of 7.6cm gun
16 air cleaner
17 V-2 12 cylinder 500hp diesel engine
18 pistol port

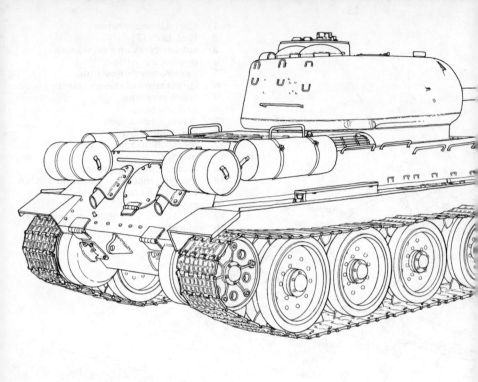

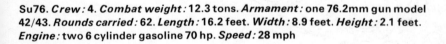

Su76. *Crew:* 4. *Combat weight:* 12.3 tons. *Armament:* one 76.2mm gun model 42/43. *Rounds carried:* 62. *Length:* 16.2 feet. *Width:* 8.9 feet. *Height:* 2.1 feet. *Engine:* two 6 cylinder gasoline 70 hp. *Speed:* 28 mph

T34/85. *Weight:* 344 tons. *Crew:* 5 men.
Armament: one 85mm gun model D-5T
(first series) of S-53 (final series) and
coaxial 7.62mm DT MG, one 7.62mm DT
MG in hull. *Rounds carried:* 85mm
56–60 rounds, 7.62mm MG 1920 rounds.
Length: 20.2 feet. *Width:* 9.9 feet.
Height: 9 feet. *Engine:* 500 hp diesel.
Speed: 33 mph. *Armour thickness:*
maximum 90mm – minimum 20 mm

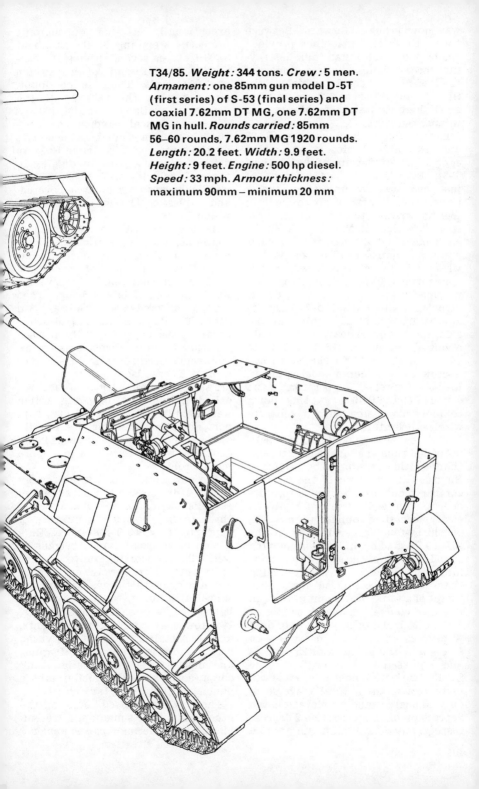

was now brought forward. Between them, these two machines provided the bulk of the Russian tank-destroying force during the remainder of the war. A third vehicle, the SU-122, mounted a 122mm gun of good high-explosive capability for infantry support.

Except for their guns, the SU-85 and the SU-100 closely resembled each other, as offspring of the 'mother' T-34. Both had a battle-weight of just over twenty-nine tons, and a power-weight ratio of approximately 16.9 horsepower to the ton – a little less than that of the early T-34. On each machine, the fighting compartment was built ahead of the engine, where the turret was fitted on the conventional T-34. This fighting compartment was housed in a superstructure, which was sloped 50 degrees at the front and 20 degrees at the side, and was quite heavily armoured – about 45mm on the SU-85 and up to 78mm on the SU-100. The SU-85 had a crew of five: commander, gunner, loader, wireless operator, and driver. The SU-100 cut this down to four, dispensing with a separate wireless operator.

The loader's task in these self-propelled guns was considerably easier than in either version of the T-34 tank. He stood in the back of the fighting compartment, and around him, clipped to the walls, were forty-eight easily-accessible rounds in the SU-85, or thirty-four larger rounds in the SU-100. He had no difficulty in moving round the rear of the gun, which made for a very much faster rate of loading than could be achieved inside the turret of a tank. Movement of the gun itself, of course, was very restricted. The SU-85 had a total traverse of only 20 degrees – that is, 10 degrees each side – and an elevation of 25 degrees and depression of 5 degrees. The SU-100, with its longer gun, was even more restricted: a total traverse of only 16 degrees and an elevation and depression of 17 degrees and 2 degrees respectively. The 100mm gun fired an exceptionally heavy armour-piercing projectile weighing 34 lbs at about 3,000 feet per second, giving it penetrative capability of roughly 160mm at 1,000 yards. There is no doubt, however, that the very small gun depression available to the SU-100 was a severe tactical handicap on even slightly-uneven ground, and accounts for the strong predilection of Russian defence zone planners for digging in their SU vehicles, with an extremely precise programme of area covered, and tables of the exact ranges at which to fire.

As the new SU vehicles became available, they were allotted a firm place in the Russian armoured formations. The organisation of armour was itself again changing in nature towards the end of 1942 – changes that rapidly gathered pace in the next two years. The Russian tank brigades now began to be experimentally massed together in larger formations – tank and mechanised corps, and even tank armies. There also began to be a line drawn once more between the so-called independent brigades, which were used in the role of infantry support, and other tank brigades, usually at the disposal of army or corps headquarters, which were used in a more mobile role.

The new tank corps was extremely variable in size. At its maximum establishment, it was made up of three tank brigades – a mixture of approximately 300 T-34s and KV-Is – with a motorised infantry brigade as well. The supporting units of this optimum tank corps were very strong: a motor cycle battalion, a reconnaissance battalion, up to two heavy tank battalions, two assault gun regiments, two towed anti-tank gun regiments, and a battalion each of Katyusha rocket launchers, anti-aircraft guns, and mortars. Thus a Russian tank corps was to provide the mobile infantry punch to follow up the tank corps.

The new mechanised corps, on the other hand, bore some family resemblance to a German *panzergrenadier* motorised division. It was established like the tank corps, but with the tank and infantry components reversed: in other words, it had three lorried infantry brigades, each with its own tank battalion, and only one tank brigade. The role of the mechanised corps was to provide the mobile infantry punch to follow up the tank corps.

Meanwhile, the independent tank brigades, during the last two years of the war, were beginning to increase in tank strength, eventually reaching a maximum of 107 T-34s per brigade. The SU machines were allotted to special support regiments, which were parcelled out to assist in operations as required. When they were being used for direct artillery support, the SU-85s and SU-100s followed up the assault waves of tanks and shock infantry, their task being to eliminate enemy points of resistance that had escaped attention by the leading wave of Russian tanks.

There was one further type of Russian armoured formation. This was the heavy tank regiment, which had a small establishment of twenty-three KV-Is, or, later, of the new Russian 'heavy', the Stalin or JS model. The Stalin was a 64-ton tank, built on the basic KV chassis. It mounted the 122mm gun, was armoured up to a thickness of 110mm, and could reach 20 miles an hour. The 122mm gun was a formidable weapon which could fire a 40 lb shot at a muzzle velocity of 2,900 feet per second. The JS-1 was followed by the JS-2, an improved version which had armour up to 160mm, and eventually, towards the end of the war, by the JS-3. This last model managed to increase its speed to twenty-three miles an hour, in spite of the fact that the armour reached 200mm.

These heavy tank regiments were used for infantry support, or in a breakthrough role if needed. In this role they were complemented by the last and biggest of, the SU series, the SU-152, which was the Russian 152mm gun-howitzer mounted on a KV chassis. Its success with the German Tiger and Panther tanks led it to be dubbed 'the animal killer' by the Russian infantry.

While all this various equipment was progressively coming into service, the Russian command in general – and Zhukov in particular – were feeling their way towards a distinctive technique in handling armour. Not for them, however, the dominant calvary *ethos* of the early panzer divisions: Zhukov's kind of armoured battle was in some ways closer in spirit to an attack on the Hindenburg Line in 1918 than to Kleist's dash to the Caucasus. German tactics, too, were changing, but not in quite the same way, for the Germans still relied upon their excellence of training and *esprit de corps* to see them through, even when they were below strength in numbers, whereas the Russians equally determined, relied in attack upon mass and in defence upon depth. Thus the year 1943 was one of probation for the Russian armour. Yet it was marked by the greatest armoured battle in the history of the world – the German assault upon Kursk. (The detailed story has been told in *Kursk* by Geoffrey Jukes, Campaign Book No. 7 in this series.) Its implications for Russian armour were considerable, because after this battle the German panzer arm could never again be considered to be an offensive strategic weapon.

By April 1943, the situation on the Eastern Front had Hitler in two minds. The catastrophe of Stalingrad had come and gone, but in March, Manstein – using the new Tigers brilliantly – had defeated the Russians round Kharkov with fine armoured tactics. His tanks had successfully manoeuvred to hit the Russians when they were themselves overstrained during their first tentative experiments with a war of movement, much as the Germans had been overstrained during the summers of 1941 and 1942.

Above: SU-122 on T-34 chassis *Below:* The Marder III: a captured 76.2mm Russian gun on the Czech 38t chassis

Above: SU-152 Russian self-propelled gun on KV chassis. *Below:*
The Czech 38t.

Manstein's success had gone far to re-establish for the moment at any rate, the moral ascendancy which the German panzers still had over their Russian counterparts. The new OKH Chief of Staff, General Kurt Zeitzler – he had replaced Halder in September 1942 – was eager to ram this advantage home. Backed at first by Manstein, he put forward a proposal to attack the great Russian salient which swelled to the west between Kharkov and Orel, and which had not been eliminated by Manstein's success of March. This salient was about 150 miles long at its base, with the city of Kursk at its centre. In it, Zeitzler reckoned, were the cream of the Russian divisions and the bulk of Russian armour.

His plan was simple. It involved two converging pincers: Model's Ninth Army, of Kluge's Army Group Centre, striking down from the north, to meet Hoth's Fourth Panzer Army, of Manstein's Army Group South, hooking up from the south. It was the kind of armoured operation, drawing a noose round the traditionally astronomical bag of Russian tanks and men, that the German panzer forces had carried out several times before. However, it faced unusual difficulties. The German tank force, which was then being comprehensively re-organised both in organisation and equipment by Guderian, was not ready; speed was vital if the operation was to be carried out in time to surprise the Russians; the Russians themselves had made considerable strides in defensive anti-tank tactics since 1941; and, finally, the Russian command was in the hands of Zhukov, who understood the nature of defence better than any other soldier of his day, and who also knew how to hold back – and when to commit – a powerful armoured reserve.

For weeks, Hitler hesitated while the argument raged among his generals – not knowing that the entire German plan had already been confided to the Russian command by the celebrated 'Lucy' spy network run by an anti-Nazi publisher in Switzerland. Finally, Hitler decided to attack, and the Kursk offensive began on July 5th, much later than Manstein had originally desired.

In the event, it proved to be a battle in the style of Zhukov rather than of Manstein. The Germans committed practically all of their painfully built-up armoured reserve, including strong detachments of the new Panthers, which were not ready for action and had a dismal baptism of breakdown and self-combustion. Zhukov, in the tactics which he had adopted in 1941, planned to receive and wear down the German attack in exceptionally deep defensive zones, where the German tanks would be progressively mauled to a standstill before they could achieve a break-through. Then, with Hoth's and Model's armour safely written down, he would begin a great armoured counterstroke at Orel and Belgorod, to the north and south of the salient respectively. He was actually superior in armour as the offensive began: on his own reckoning, he had about 3,600 tanks and SU machines, giving him a ratio in his favour of about 1.3 to 1. This, however, was a general superiority, and included his armoured reserve. In some areas during the early fighting, at any rate, the Germans were certain to achieve local superiorities of up to 6 to 1.

The offensive armoured tactics used by the Germans at Kursk and the defensive methods adopted by the Russians reveal how much tank warfare had already changed. The German technique was known as the *panzerkeil*. Under this system, the heaviest armour, the Tigers or heaviest self-propelled guns, formed the tip of a wedge, with the more lightly-armoured Panthers and Mark IVs deployed behind them, with their following infantry. Thus the breakthrough would be effected by the tanks which could both deal and receive the heaviest blows, after which the faster tanks would exploit.

Above: Field-Marshal Eric von Manstein. *Below:* German assault gun outside Kharkov

Above: Panzer grenadiers on the steppe.
Left: German infantry under a
knocked-out Russian tank. Note
egg-shaped grenades

The Russian defensive tactics reflected the growing strength of anti-
tank measures. Their system was, in
fact, adapted from one used by the
Germans, by whom it was known as a
pakfront. In the Russian version of
this, up to ten anti-tank guns –
usually the 76.2mm which had difficulty in dealing with the Tiger – were
arranged under the command of one
officer, who could thus bring down a
storm of anti-tank fire upon a single
target. The *pakfronts* in the Kursk
Salient were all carefully sited in
great depth, so that even when German
tanks had forced their way through
one belt, they were sure to be attacked
in flank by another. In addition, the
pakfronts were surrounded by mines,
which were used by the Russians on
an enormous scale. The German
command estimated that the enemy

was able to lay 30,000 mines in forty-
eight hours, and that any German
corps could count on lifting 40,000
a day. The defensive web of the
pakfronts was hidden by excellent
Russian camouflage. 'Neither mine-
fields or *pakfronts*,' said a German
tank officer, 'could be detected until
the first tank blew up, or the first
Russian anti-tank gun opened fire ...'

It is abundantly clear that this
kind of warfare suited Zhukov much
better than it suited Hoth. Mass was
the weapon, in depth for both attack
and defence. Against this, the panzer
divisions would launch themselves
in vain. One panzer staff opinion
summed up the whole affair trench-
antly: '... The German army threw
away all its advantages in mobile
war, and met the Russians on ground
of their own choosing ... the German
command could think of nothing
better to do than to fling our mag-
nificent panzer divisions against the
strongest fortress in the world ...'

It was true that Kursk *was* a twen-
tieth century fortress, and Hitler had
already recognised that it would need
a special weapon. He had chosen as his
fortress-breaker the ultimate self-
propelled gun of its day, a dinosaur-
like monster known variously as the
Ferdinand (after its creator, Dr
Ferdinand Porsche) or, at the front,
as the *Elefant*. This extraordinary
machine, which was based on an
original Porsche design for the Tiger,
weighed seventy tons, and had armour
of up to 200mm – that is to say, thicker
than that on some of the British
battlecruisers which fought at
Jutland. It was armed with the
superb 88m L71 gun, which could
penetrate 182mm of armour at 500
yards. However, it had no secondary
machine gun armament – a curious
omission which, in the battle of
Kursk – was to doom its crews to an
unpleasant death. The *Elefant* itself,
and its place in the German assaulting
force, were added evidence of the retreat of tank warfare from the carefree
cavalry days of the recent past.

Above: German Mark IV with circular supplementary on turret and skirts on hull to counter hollow charge weapons. *Left:* The Germans take over a Russian trench, ignoring their conquests *Below:* German *sturmgeschutz* (7.5cm)

The defence of the Kursk Salient involved four other Russian commanders apart from Zhukov, who was the overall co-ordinator. North-east of Kursk, Rokossovsky commanded the Central Front – a Soviet 'front' being roughly comparable to a British or American army group. Rokossovsky's troops would meet the attack by Model's Ninth Army – an attack which was to be reinforced by ninety of the giant Porsche *Elefants*. South of Kursk, Vatutin, commanding the Voronezh Front, would receive the assault of Hoth's Fourth Panzer Army. Behind both Central and Voronezh Fronts stood the Russian operational reserve, commanded by Koniev. This force was especially strong in armour, and included Rotmistrov's Fifth Guards Tank Army

Left: Tiger I with Mark IIIs. *Below:* Kursk, 1943: Sturmovik ground strafer aircraft clear the way for Russian armour

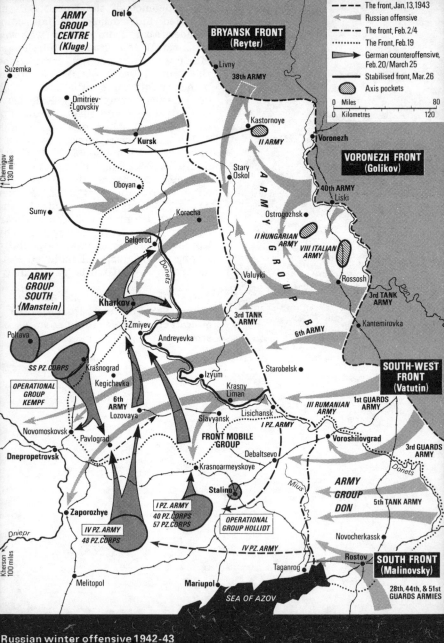

Legend	
– – –	The front, Jan. 13, 1943
	Russian offensive
– · – · –	The front, Feb. 2/4
	The Front, Feb. 19
	German counteroffensive, Feb. 20/March 25
	Stabilised front, Mar. 26
	Axis pockets

0 Miles 80
0 Kilometres 120

ARMY GROUP CENTRE (Kluge)

Orel

Suzemka

Dmitriev-Lgovskiy

Chernigov ← 130 miles

Kursk

Oboyan

Sumy

BRYANSK FRONT (Reyter)

Livny

38th ARMY

Kastornoye

II ARMY

Voronezh

Stary Oskol

VORONEZH FRONT (Golikov)

40th ARMY

Liski

Ostrogozhsk

II HUNGARIAN ARMY

VIII ITALIAN ARMY

Rossosh

3rd TANK ARMY

Kantemirovka

Belgorod

Korocha

Valuyki

A R M Y   G R O U P   B

Donets

ARMY GROUP SOUTH (Manstein)

Kharkov

Zmiyev

Andreyevka

3rd TANK ARMY

6th ARMY

SOUTH-WEST FRONT (Vatutin)

Poltava

SS PZ. CORPS

Krasnograd

Kegichevka

6th ARMY

Lozovaya

OPERATIONAL GROUP KEMPF

Izyum

Krasny Liman

Starobelsk

III RUMANIAN ARMY

1st GUARDS ARMY

Novomoskovsk

Pavlograd

Slavyansk

Lisichansk

I PZ. ARMY

FRONT MOBILE GROUP

Debaltsevo

Voroshilovgrad

3rd GUARDS ARMY

Dnepr

Dnepropetrovsk

Krasnoarmeyskoye

Stalino

I PZ. ARMY
40 PZ. CORPS
57 PZ. CORPS

OPERATIONAL GROUP HOLLIDT

Mius

Donets

ARMY GROUP DON

5th TANK ARMY

Zaporozhye

IV PZ. ARMY
48 PZ. CORPS

Novocherkassk

Kherson 100 miles

IV PZ. ARMY

Rostov

SOUTH FRONT (Malinovsky)

Melitopol

Taganrog

Mariupol

28th, 44th, & 51st GUARDS ARMIES

SEA OF AZOV

Russian winter offensive 1942–43

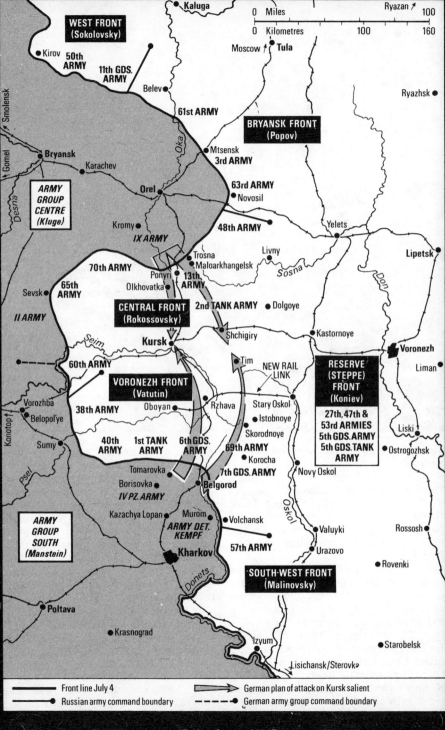

Plan of German counterattack on Bulge formed by Russian offensive

The dinosaurs of Kursk: knocked-out Porsche Elefants

the I Guards Mechanised Corps, the IV Guards Tank Corps, and the X Tank Corps. It was, indeed, a mass of tanks which included some of the elite armoured formations of the Red Army.

When it was used in battle, under a tightly-controlling hand, it would have a devastating effect. The whole of Koniev's command, and especially his armour, was planned to have a role far exceeding that of earlier Russian reserve fronts, which had often been little more than second, third or fourth lines of defence. Koniev's tanks and troops were a true reserve in the classic military sense –

a decision-achieving force whose task was not only to smash up any successful local German breakthrough, but also to move up from the Russian rear areas as a reinforcing counter-punch when the Russian's own offensive began. In the event, as will be seen, Zhukov somewhat under-estimated the inroads on the armoured reserve which would be made by the sheer task of defeating the German panzers inside the Salient, and Koniev was not able immediately to carry out his full task of pursuit and destruction.

The stakes for the Russians at Kursk were enormous. The forces in and around the Salient amounted to 3,600 tanks, 20,000 guns, 1,300,000 men, and 2,400 aircraft. This was the equivalent of roughly a fifth of the

entire contemporary strength of the Red Army in men and guns, more than a third of its available tanks, and a quarter of its aircraft. For the Germans, however, the risk was even greater – nothing less than the bulk of their equipment and the carefully built-up morale of the precious panzer forces that Guderian had reconstituted during his short time as Inspector General of Armoured Troops. Without the panzer arm, Hitler could not win the war. At Kursk he put it, finally, to fatal risk.

Doom lay heavy on the operation – codenamed *Zitadelle* – from the beginning. Model's attack in the north was ground to a standstill by Rokossovsky's *pakfronts*. This was not surprising when it is remembered that Rokossovsky's Front alone contained more than 3,000 miles of trench, and 400,000 mines, giving a total of 2,400 anti-tank and 2,700 anti-personnel mines to each mile of front – about four times the defensive scale achieved at Stalingrad. Some sectors had more than 150 large guns and mortars to the mile. The German tank crews found themselves inside a panzer Verdun.

Moreover, the ninety Porsche *Elefants* proved a sad disappointment when the attempt was made to ignore their tactical limitations and use them as tanks. Waddling invulnerably through the storm of frontal fire, they were picked off one by one by dug-in Russian armour on the flanks, or knocked out by determined Russian infantry against whom they had no

The man who showed the way: General Katukov

Austere, unassuming, ambitious: Marshal Ivan Koniev

machine gun defence. Guderian said contemptuously that they were 'quail shooting with cannon . . .'

Meanwhile, in the south, Hoth's Fourth Panzer Army, with the bulk of the German armour, fought magnificently according to the high panzer tradition. The German numbers here seemed overwhelming to the Russians at first. Around Oboyan, fifty miles south of Kursk, a Russian general watched the enemy tanks come rumbling on and recorded later that 'I suppose that neither I nor any of our other officers had ever seen so many enemy tanks at once. Hoth had staked everything on a knight's move. Against every one of our companies of ten tanks were thirty or forty German tanks. Hoth well knew that if he could break through to Kursk, no losses would be too great and no sacrifice would be in vain . . .'

It is clear from this that Zhukov himself was to some extent gambling, hoping that though inside the salient the Russians were in some places heavily outnumbered, tank against tank, nevertheless the *pakfronts* and the mines would take sufficient toll of Fourth Panzer Army to allow him to continue to hold back Koniev's armoured reserve. The battle had opened on 5th July, but the true crisis did not come for a week. By then Hoth, in spite of seven days in which he had moved forward about twelve miles and inflicted very heavy losses on the Russian T-34s, was in an unenviable position. In the north, Model was at a standstill, having already lost – according to Russian estimates – about 200 tanks and 25,000 men in killed and wounded. Thus Model was unable to protect Hoth from the mounting pressure on the left flank of Fourth Panzer Army – and Hoth's own losses were growing day by day. Hoth now decided to break through to the area around Prokhorovka, a little southeast of Oboyan, where there was more open country, and where he would himself be placed to deliver a blow at the Russian left and rear.

Kursk, 1943: Drokhorovka – a victorious Russian tank crew which disputed Fourth Panzer Army's death ride

Vatutin had already committed the armoured reserve of his own Front on 6th July. This was Katukov's First Tank Army, which consisted of one mechanised and two tank corps. Katukov had suffered even more heavily than the Germans in a confused tank battle south of Oboyan, and had finally ordered that a good proportion of his surviving tanks should be dug in as static firing points. Thus Hoth's decision to move on Prokhorovka caught Vatutin – and Katukov's armour – at a difficult moment, low in numbers and restricted in mobility. Hoth's Fourth Panzer Army, in spite of its own losses, was still a very formidable force, amounting to around 600 Panthers, Tigers, Mark IVs, and self-propelled guns. It was clear that this would be the turning point of the battle.

The Russian command could delay no longer in bringing Koniev's armour into play, although the time for this had come sooner than had been originally planned. Hoth's move to Prokhorovka must be turned from a side-stepping knight's move to a death ride. Zhukov now drew from Koniev's reserve front Rotmistrov's Fifth Guards Tank Army.

As Hoth's panzers came into sight, trailing their thick dust clouds in the early morning sun, Rotmistrov's T-34s took them in the flank, passing diagonally through the lines of German tanks at point-blank range, in the style of an old-fashioned cavalry charge. Never before or since have tanks been used in this way on this scale. More than 1,500 machines were milling on the steppe in a confused, dust-shrouded mass, thickened by the billowing black, oily smoke from stricken tanks and guns. The Tigers and Panthers, taken at ranges of often under one hundred yards, found that at these desperately close quarters even the 76.2mm guns on the T-34s could pierce and destroy them, although the long, higher-velocity guns on the German tanks did dreadful execution. When night came, the darkness was lit by the sparks and swirling flame from hundred upon hundred of blazing tanks and self-propelled guns, or from the wreckage

Above: The German flail: a squadron of Stukas. *Below:* The Russian hammer: the armoured Shturmovik

of scores of the German *Stuka* dive-bombers or Russian *Shturmovik* tank-busting aircraft which had ranged over the battlefield, adding their own tallies of death and destruction to the holocaust below. The Russian command estimated that this day alone cost Hoth 350 tanks and more than 10,000 men in tank crews and support ing infantry. No accurate estimate of Russian losses is available, but they, too, must have been staggering.

However, far away in OKW, Hitler was already calling off *Zitadelle* more because he needed reinforcements to deal with the Allied landing in Sicily than from any clear understanding of what had happened at Kursk. For from this day forward, the panzer arm, though not yet shattered, would never recover: henceforth the initiative in armoured warfare would lie with the Russians. Their self-confidence had received a vital boost. Zhukov summed up with his usual clear-sightedness:

'In the Kursk counter-offensive, we used special mechanised and tank units widely for the first time, and in several operations and manoeuvres they were the decisive factor, penetrating the enemy lines in depth and driving wedges into the rear of enemy groupings. The tank armies . . . essentially changed our capabilities, and consequently the character of front operations, not only in scale but also in objectives. In comparison with the first period of the war, Soviet forces became far more mobile . . . The density of artillery and tanks per mile of front was sharply raised. In the summer offensive we found it possible to create a density of 250 to 300 guns and twenty-five to thirty tanks per mile . . .'

This counter-offensive, of course, was the second stage of Zhukov's plan. It began earlier in the north, around Orel, than in the south. Rokossovsky's forces went over to the offensive on 12th July, but Vatutin's Voronezh Front, supported by Koniev's Reserve Front, did not really get going until 3rd August. This was undoubtedly because a large part of Koniev's armour – Rotmistrov's Fifth Guards Tank Army – had been necessarily expended in the tremendous battle at Prokhorovka. Thus Koniev lacked tanks for the steel tip of his counter-thrust.

There was also a typically-Zhukov element of deliberation in the whole conception of the counter-offensive. The troops in the north had already meticulously planned their own part in it, and all supplies and communications had been carefully prepared. In the south, where Hoth's panzers had caused more disruption, and where the battle had been much more of a close-run thing, the plans for the counter-attack had been disrupted when Koniev's tanks had been prematurely drawn into action, so that Russian troops were not ready quite as quickly for the next moves. One cannot imagine Hoth, Guderian, or Kleist having to reorganise quite so ponderously, and the delay until 3rd August is a reminder that Russian armour was not yet as flexible an instrument as the German panzer force, and that Zhukov, by necessity as well as by nature, had to keep a tight hand on his tanks.

However, once the southern wing of the counter-offensive began to roll, it made spectacular progress against the weakened German forces, capturing Belgorod on 5th August and Kharkov itself on the 23rd. During September, the whole of the Donets Basin was cleared, and by the 22nd of that month Russian tanks – the Third Guards Tank Army, commanded by General P S Rybalko, which was part of Vatutin's Voronezh Front – reached the banks of the Dniepr river at Kanev. In Russian as well as in German eyes, this was a climactic moment. From now on, steady and relentless – though interrupted at intervals by the fine generalship and the dogged courage of the German panzers – the pursuit which would end in Berlin in the spring of 1945 had at last begun.

The reward

By 1944, slowly and bloodily, the Russian armour had been changed from a bludgeon into a broadsword. In general, the quality of tank crews was rising to a level which was acceptable for armoured operations of a more daring type than the infantry support actions of the past. There were still gaps, of course, as was inevitable with a force so rapidly expanded under the pressure of a gigantic national crisis. As late as December 1943, German troops near Zhitomir captured Russian tank crews who appeared to have had little or no training: one tank commander told his interrogators that only a month ago he had been working at a factory in the Urals. A proclamation from Stalin had been read to the assembled workers, calling for anyone capable of operating a tank to join the Red Army immediately. Within three weeks, he had been in battle. This, however, can only have been an exception. There was to be plenty of evidence during the spring of 1944 that the Russian tanks were manned by crews who, though their spirit was of a different kind from that which had imbued the German panzer troops earlier in the war, nevertheless were now beginning to understand the new nature of armoured conflict, and to make their own distinctive and decisive contribution to it.

If the instrument was getting sharper, the men who wielded it were getting better. Confidence in battle seeps down from the top, and in the Red Army the crucible of war had now moulded two leaders capable of taking their place among the great captains of history, and who, had they been Germans, would have held commands as high under Hitler as they did under Stalin. One of these, of course, was Georgi Zhukov. The other was Ivan Koniev. They were men of vastly different temperament, but their shared ambitions gave them a mutual

T34s and infantry move towards the front

125

Left: A knocked out T34 adds to the debris of war. *Above:* German assault guns in winter camouflage

antipathy. This was exacerbated by their rival claims for glory, and the fact that Koniev was an admirer of Stalin's military qualities, while Zhukov's very nature gave him a more riskily-independent view.

Zhukov, both to his fellow commanders and to his subordinates, must have seemed more like a demon than a man. He was ruthless to the point of caricature: his arrival at a threatened point in the front meant wholesale threats of the firing squad for those who did not do their duty as he saw it, and of instant dismissal for those who argued. His mind, however, was brilliant: he had the *coup de l'oeil*, the ability to read a battle, which was shared on the Allied side by Montgomery, Slim, and MacArthur, and on the German by Rommel and Manstein. Handling his enormous bodies of men – ten, fifteen or twenty

armies at a time, with thousands of tanks and aircraft – Zhukov could spare no self-identification with the fate of individual units, as British commanders could with Scottish or London divisions, or the Germans with elite formations which were the pride of the panzer armies. Zhukov knew that the counter-weight to the German armies was blood, and he weighted the scales with blood until they tipped to his advantage. He had learned, instinctively and clearly, that the arts of defence once more ruled the battlefield, that a successful offensive must always be preceded by a successful defensive, and that the weapon for such a victory was the tank arm of the Red Army – provided that the Russian tanks did not allow themselves to be drawn into the old, fatal cavalry error of over-stretch. The three basic Russian tanks between them provided an almost ideal instrument for Zhukov's conception of battle, which was now to come to its full fruition.

Ivan Koniev was a man of a very different kind, showing the austere and modest characteristics of a Stonewall Jackson rather than the imperious energy of a Zhukov. In 1944, he was forty-eight, a soldier of great experience who had served in Siberia during the Civil War. He was liked by his staffs, who respected both his unassuming habits – he often wore a cloak at the front to conceal his rank in case it should embarrass the troops – and his flair for battle. Koniev drank no alcohol, and carried with him a small case of books – Livy, Tolstoy, Pushkin, Gogol. Behind his spectacles, his mind was sharp: he expected a great deal from his staff and his junior commanders, and his anger, when it came, could be formidable. He looked up to Stalin: he would read a Stalin-drafted order from *Stavka* and loyally exclaim: 'That's the way to write. Everything fits. There's *thought* behind every word . . .' This man was now to deal a savage blow to the best commander in the German army – a

Above: A knocked out Russian KV tank.
Right: A knocked out Russian T34 put to effective use as a strong-point by German troops

blow which would finally convince the Russian armour, already vindicated defensively by its success at Kursk, of its capacity to take on and defeat the Germans in techniques of armoured attack.

The Russians, in fact, were presented with an opportunity to achieve a small-scale Stalingrad on the Dniepr in January 1944. This chance arose because of Hitler's insistence that Manstein's Army Group South should give no ground in the bend of the great river, which left ten somewhat understrength German divisions grouped around Korsun, about 120 miles south-east of Zhitomir. These divisions were from the First Panzer and Eighth Armies. They were now being threatened by two converging pincers – to the north, by the army group under Vatutin, now known as

the First Ukrainian Front, and to the south by Koniev's command, which had been re-christened the Second Ukrainian Front. Koniev's advance had caught Manstein in an unenviable position. His tank reserves were largely drained away, and he had no effective means of holding open a route for the escape or the reinforcement of the beleagured divisions – one of which was the once-formidable SS *Viking*.

Koniev's force included Rotmistrov's Fifth Guards Tank Army, now refurbished after its great struggle in the Kursk Salient. The right-hand wing of his army group drove into the German bulge on the Dniepr on 24th January, inserting a tank-infantry wedge some eight miles deep and seventeen miles wide. Two days later, Vatutin's forces also advanced from the north, and on the 28th the two Russian pincers closed at Zvenigorodka. The ten German divisions were trapped in just such a noose as similar Russian formations had found themselves inside at the opening of *Barbarossa*. This time, however, the trapped forces were given little opportunity to filter out. Using the scanty remnant of his panzers, Manstein attempted to hold open a corridor to the south. At this point, Koniev sent in Rotmistrov's T-34s to play the role of destructive cavalry. Indeed, the situation so called for this move that the Russian command actually supported Rotmistrov with a cavalry division, so that horsemen with sabres moved among the racing lines of tanks. A Belgian eyewitness who was in the Korsun pocket with the SS *Wallonia* brigade described later the appalling scenes as Rotmistrov's tanks moved on the German columns attempting to pass south down the corridor. The T-34s advanced in waves crushing supply wagons and guns beneath their tracks as they literally drove over the retreating Germans. When the Germans reached a stream, many soldiers tore off their clothes in an effort to get through the icy water,

while the T-34s moved down the banks, playing their Degtyarev machine guns on the swarming, struggling mass. Thousands of soldiers, some naked, others with their frozen clothing stiff on their bodies, ran through the snow until they dropped under the steady, rhythmic fire of the tanks.

Another column, also trying to break out, suffered an even more macabre fate. This was on the night of 17th February, outside the village of Shanderovka. The village had been under heavy shellfire throughout the hours of darkness, but as morning came the German troops tried to move out. They formed themselves into rough marching order, the SS men of the *Wallonia* Brigade and the *Viking* Division on the outside, with the ordinary Wehrmacht infantry in the middle. But the Russian tanks were waiting. A Soviet major described what happened:

'It was about six o'clock in the morning. Our tanks and our cavalry suddenly appeared and rushed straight into the thick of the columns . . . The Germans ran in all directions. And for the next four hours, our tanks raced up and down the plain crushing them by the hundred. Our cavalry, competing with the tanks, chased them through the ravines where it was hard for the tanks to pursue them . . . Hundreds and hundreds of cavalry were hacking at them with their sabres, and massacred the Fritzes as no one had ever been massacred by cavalry before. It was the kind of carnage that nothing could stop until it was all over. In a small area over 20,000 Germans were killed. I had been in Stalingrad, but never had I seen such concentrated slaughter . . .'

Between them, Koniev and his tank lieutenant Rotmistrov had scored an immense psychological victory. They had demonstrated that Russian armour could exploit, encircle and destroy – a lesson not only for their own men but also for the Germans. From now forward, no German formation could

Above: German 8.8mm flak positions. *Below:* A German observation post

General Vatutin

shrug off the chance of a similar envelopment. For Manstein, of course, it was the beginning of the end. The battle of Korsun meant that he could no longer hold up Koniev's drive. For Koniev, it meant promotion to the rank of marshal.

Meanwhile, the command of the First Ukrainian Front changed. Vatutin was ambushed in his staff car by anti-communist partisans on 1st March, and died of his wounds a few weeks later. Sensing that great things were beginning to happen in the Ukraine, Zhukov himself took operational control of Vatutin's armies, while Koniev began the armoured drive which the Russians call 'the *blitzkrieg* through the mud.' It is an interesting technical reflection that this crucial advance was possible *only* because of the broad tracks and formidable automotive qualities of the T-34: observers at the front noted that of all the tanks available, both German and Russian, only the T-34 could move effectively through the swampy wastelands of the early spring, supported by the excellent four-wheel-drive Studebaker trucks of which thousands were being sup-

plied from the United States. The Russian artillery was nearly as immobile as its German counterpart. The offensive, as it moved forward, had to be conducted by T-34s and SUs supported by infantry, but without conventional guns.

However, it began with an artillery barrage of great power and weight. Then the tanks and the SUs moved forward, in the now-familiar Russian technique. This meant that formations of 200 or 300 tanks would be massed on a front of less than a mile, moving in three waves. The tanks in the last two waves often had infantry clinging to their backs and sides. This was an unsatisfactory substitute for proper armoured troop carriers, since not only did infantry on the outside of the tank seriously impede the laying and firing of the gun, but the infantrymen themselves were also highly vulnerable to determined German machine gun fire.

Once the leading tanks had made a wide enough breach in the German defences, more tanks – these were almost invariably T-34s – would pour through the hole to complete the work of destruction, and make the way clear for the next bound of the whole combined force.

These tactics, it will be seen, depended on mass. Like all tactics involving mass, they were costly. The courage and determination of the German panzer crews, even when, as was increasingly the case, they were *in extremis*, helped them to play the desperate role of the German rapier against the Russian broadsword. In this role, they imposed a heavy bill upon the Russian armour. The war diaries of German divisions are full of small, bloody encounters, tank ambushes in Ukrainian forest, flank-traps set by *jagdpanzers* in villages and hamlets, in which considerable numbers of Russian tanks were left burning, for the loss of half as many German machines

Every German loss, however, meant that the panzer arm was bleeding to

Panzer IV crews in an off-duty moment

death. German production was simply not adequate to supply the needs of all the fronts, whereas the Russian outflow of machines was now reaching its height. A glance at German production statistics for 1944–45 tells its own story: tank manufacture reached nearly 8,400, of which 3,366 were Mark IVs, 3,965 were Panthers, 623 were Tiger Is and 377 were Tiger IIs. In addition, there were 3,617 *jagdpanzers* and 5,751 mobile assault guns.

The Russian production figures are startlingly more impressive. The great upheaval of 1941 was now long over. From the Urals, the T-34 chassis alone was being produced at the rate of well over 20,000 a year – about half of those finally becoming T-34/85 tanks, and the rest made up of various types of US assault guns and tank destroyers. The total Russian production of tanks, SUs and armoured cars in 1944 was roughly 30,000. When it is remembered that in the spring of 1944, Germany was already holding panzer and panzergrenadier divisions in Italy on her much smaller 'second front', and that in three months she was to be involved in another great

struggle in the West, taking on the enormous combined tank factory facilities of the United States and Britain, it is clear that inadequate tank production alone was sufficient to lose her the war. In other than human terms, Koniev and Zhukov could afford to pay a stiff price for every Mark IV, Tiger, or Panther that they destroyed.

Koniev's offensive burst into life on 5th March. By the 11th, his tanks had seized Uman, and within a fortnight they had reached the line of the Bug river, which up to that point had formed the demarcation line between the occupation zones in Russia of Germany and Rumania. German prisoners showed unusually poor morale – a direct result, observers noted, of Koniev's victory at Korsun.

By 26th March, a climactic moment had arrived. Koniev forced successively the Dniester and Prut rivers, and his troops drove for the first time out of Russia and into an enemy land, seizing a large bulge of Rumanian territory. Behind Koniev, nearly all

133

Above: Those who fell: a dead infantryman, a knocked out T34. *Below:* A Panzer IV carries infantry into battle. *Right:* General Manteuffel, left, consults one of his officers

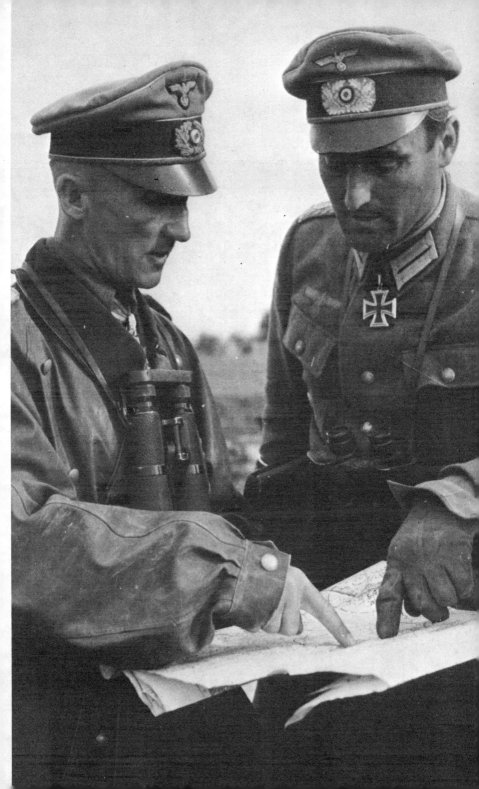

Above: A British made Valentine tank, and Cossack troops in an attack. *Left:* German assault gun and infantry patrol

the Ukraine was back in Russian hands. Farther west, two celebrated German commanders stood before Hitler. Courteously, the Führer awarded to Manstein and Kleist the Swords to their Knight's Cross. Then they were relieved of their commands – Model, for the moment, taking over Manstein's Army. Group South. Taking into account the fact that Hoth of Fourth Panzer Army had been dismissed a little earlier, Zhukov and Koniev had scored a remarkable personal and psychological victory, eliminating three of their most experienced and formidable opponents at one stroke.

Koniev's armour had done its job superbly, although its losses had been heavy. Again and again, the retreating Germans, turning and striking swiftly, using their still-considerable superiority in tactics and training, had managed to inflict stinging wounds on the Russian tank armies – but never sufficiently seriously to check their remorseless advance. Manteuffel, who was to command the *Gross Deutschland* division for part of the Russian campaign, has described the advance of the Russian tanks as 'something that Westerners cannot imagine . . .' He saw it as a mass of men pressing on behind the tank vanguard, many of them – as, indeed, in the German armies – mounted on horseback or driving horse-pulled wagons. On the backs of the Russian infantry were sacks of dry crusts or vegetables plucked from the villages and hamlets passed through during the march. The horses got little more to eat than the straw from the roofs of peasant cottages. Allowing for a certain amount of emotive licence in this description – the Germans were always prone to present themselves as a civilised bastion of the West overwhelmed by unshaven hordes from Tartary – one can see that the very lack of supply establishment in the Russian armies presented a tactical problem for the Germans. All the Russian armoured columns ap-

peared to need was fuel and ammunition: the infantry looked after themselves. It was somewhat disconcerting to plan tactical moves which nipped into a flank to cut off enemy supplies – and then find there were no supplies worth speaking of.

After the clearing of the Ukraine, the Russian armies began to regroup for their greatest offensive of all, which was to end in the destruction of Army Group Centre, carrying the Russian tanks to the Vistula, and thence into Germany itself. At this point, it is as well to look back on what the Russian tank arm had achieved since its traumatic experiences of 1941. In enemy eyes, above all, its progress had been startling.

What impressed the Germans most about Russian armour was the sheer weight of the formations used, and the meticulous, detailed planning of each successive operation. By 1944, the days of Timoshenko's messed-up offensive outside Kharkov had gone forever. Russian commanders were far too frightened of Zhukov to try premature operations. The example of Zhukov was infectious: every Russian commander – and this applied especially to the armour – planned his battle down to the use of the last platoon or the last tank, and, like Montgomery further west, began no battle unless he was sure he would win it.

This involved careful rehearsal of every attack. The number of troops, tanks and guns for any operation was laid down rigidly in tables. This was quite alien to German practice, and at first excited their derision. Manstein, however, reviewing the Russian methods, observed sombrely that an attack might be slow in starting, 'but once begun it was expected to be carried through in one sweep. Neither the consolidation of ground nor the coming of night were allowed to stop the advance. No attack was halted until the troops had been used up and had run out of supplies . . .'

Nemesis

While the spring of 1944 hardened into summer, the Russians paused. When their new offensive opened on 22nd June – three years to the day since the German armies had launched Operation *Barbarossa* – it was spearheaded by Russian tanks in one of the most staggering blows in the history of war – an advance of 450 miles in five weeks, with the destruction of twenty-five German divisions, and the breakdown of the whole of the position of Army Group Centre. Such a blow and such a rate of advance could be achieved only by a tank arm which had learned the nature of modern war, and by generals who knew clearly how to use it.

At last, and in abundance, the tank strength for such a gigantic offensive was ready. The main weight of the attack was distributed by *Stavka* among four fronts: the First Baltic, commanded by Bagramyan; the Third Byelorussian, commanded by Chernyakovsky; the Second Byelorussian, commanded by Zakharov; and the First Byelorussian, commanded by Rokossovsky. These four fronts stretched down successively from south of Leningrad to Kovel, in the Ukraine. Between them they disposed of 2,500,000 men and forty-one armoured brigades, many of them arranged in tank armies. This was approximately three times the available German tank strength. Chernyakovsky's command included the famous Fifth Guards Tank Army, now headed by Volski, who had commanded a mechanised corps at Stalingrad. This change of command took place because the tank army's old leader, Rotmistrov, had now been promoted marshal, and had become deputy commander of the entire Russian armoured force.

By 25th June, at the northern end of the combined front, Bagramyen and Chernyakovski linked forces to take the fortress of Vitebsk from Army Group Centre, which was now com-

Josef Stalin I tanks approach Berlin

Left: A T34 that failed to negotiate a ditch. *Above:* Katyusha rockets are fired off in a barrage on the Ukranian front

manded by Busch, a veteran of the French campaign of 1940. Zakharov's front took Moglilev three days later, crossing the Dniepr with heavy casualties. Farther south still Rokossovsky's tanks encircled the remains of several Panzer divisions. By 13th July, Vilna and Minsk had been taken by Chernyakovsky, who was driving on to East Prussia, smashing his tanks through a ragged Patchwork of German defences, and delayed more by supply problems than by enemy fire. Rokossovsky, for his part, took Brest Litovsk and crossed the Vistula early in August. Thus Army Group Centre had been effectively destroyed, though the speed and scope of the Russian advance meant that a pause must now be made, since the spearhead formations were dangerously overstretched.

On the other side of the hill, there were bitter moments for the glittering panzer leaders of the recent past, headed by Guderian. The German panzers were fighting with exemplary skill and courage, but their losses were mounting, and there seemed to be an inexhaustible supply of Russian tanks and crews to replace those picked off by the shrinking companies of Panthers, Tigers, and Mark IVs. Guderian watched with a heavy heart but with professional admiration as Chernyakovsky and Rokossovsky poured on to the west. 'Shattering events . . .,' he recorded. 'It seemed as though nothing could ever stop them . . .'

However, as the Russian drive slackened after its incredible 450-mile bound, once more the German command began to shore up its cracking eastern wall, replacing Busch by Model at the head of a reconstituted Army Group Centre, which was now re-established east of Warsaw. For the Russians, the centre of their front

Above left: The German 'Hornet'
8.8cm self-propelled gun. *Left:* German
troops wait for the enemy behind a
knocked out Stalin tank. *Above:* A
British Valentine tank, used by the
Russians, knocked out, and now
employed as a strong point by German
troops. In the background are a T34,
left, and another Valentine, centre

now had to remain static as they
rebuilt communications over the
shattered territories across which the
tank armies had roamed. They paused for six months on the Vistula. On
the left flank of the Russian advance,
Rumania now fell out of the war.
Malinovsky's Second Ukrainian Front
(for Koniev had now gone to command
the First) struck out for Bucharest,
with the T-34s of Kravchenko's Sixth
Tank Army in the van. The speed and
range of the T-34 have never been
better demonstrated. Malinovsky's
tactics were Zhukov-style – a break-
in by two armies in the valley of the
Prut on 20th August, after which

Kravchenko's tank army was put
through the gap. Twelve days and
250 miles later, Kravchenko's tanks
were rumbling into the Rumanian
capital, clearing the Ploesti oilfields
on the way. It was one of the most
brilliant dashes of the war.

The confidence of Russian commanders in their handling of armour
was now producing a curious side-
effect. Gone were the days of nervous-
ness and hesitation, when sometimes
it seemed that only Zhukov had the
will-power and the demonic energy
to take the right decisions. Now the
Russian tanks were becoming the
vehicle for private ambition as well
as national victory. The furnace of
war had moulded generals who were
considerable military figures by any
standards: Zhukov himself, Koniev,
Rokossovsky, Rotmistrov, Chernyakovsky, Malinovsky, Vasilevsky, and
others. However, the writing of
history in Soviet Russia was a very
different thing from what it was
farther west, and Russian com-

Marshal Rokossovsky

Marshal Malinovsky

Marshal Zakharov

manders were well aware that they would have to fight for their places. Stalin, too, had his own ideas as to which generals should receive which particular ration of glory.

As it became steadily clearer that Hitler's crumbling empire could not hold out for more than a few more months, the jockeying for fame among the Russian senior commanders became more and more fierce. When Vasilevsky replaced the brilliant Chernyakovsky (killed by a shell in February 1945), Zhukov kept a watchful eye. One Russian corps commander was dismissed, and a divisional commander sent to a punishment battalion, because their dilly-dallying looked like giving Vasilevsky the chance to score an important success before Zhukov could register a new victory of his own.

Stalin, however, had already chosen Zhukov for the star role in the coming assault on Berlin. Planning for this had begun in October, and an enormous tank force - the bulk of it T-34s though with several battalions of JS tanks for heavy fire support - was available for the final thrust. A total of twenty-three corps and thirteen mechanised corps formed the heart of the tank strength, with, of course, other independent tank brigades parcelled out among the rifle divisions.

Two fronts were given the main role in the race into Germany, but only one was intended to capture Berlin. To achieve this, Stalin first of all eliminated Rokossovsky from the main contenders. His First Byelorussian Front was now given to Zhukov, while he himself was sent to command the Second Byelorussian Front, which had a highly-important but less charismatic role on the right wing. Rokossovsky, who seems to have been comfortably contemplating the fame that would soon be his, was indignant. He said later that he asked Stalin: 'Why am I being penalised?' He received a cold answer – merely the repetition of the order and the instruction that he could find out

all he needed to know at headquarters.

To the south of Zhukov, and in a necessarily vital role, was Koniev's First Ukrainian Front. Between them, Zhukov and Koniev disposed of 45 per cent of the men, 70 per cent of the armour, and 43 per cent of the guns of the Red Army. They shared six tank armies – some of them formations which had won fame in earlier operations. Zhukov had two of the elite Guards Tank Armies. One of these, the First, was commanded by the brilliant Katukov.

This was no accident. Stalin had decided that Zhukov, and only Zhukov, should capture Berlin. In his role as co-ordinator of the efforts of the various fronts he established – at a conference on 15th November – zones of activity which meant that Koniev would be kept out of the city until Zhukov had firmly established his claim to be its conqueror. War, however, is not a completely exact science, even for a Zhukov. Koniev was far too experienced, determined and skilful, and his forces were far too near, to be pushed aside so easily. He intended, when the time came, to be in at the kill. After the war, Zhukov himself showed how clearly he had realised this. 'As for our neighbour on the south,' he recorded drily, 'we were confident he would not lag behind . . .'

Koniev attacked first, on 12th January, breaking out of the Russian bridgehead on the Vistula near Sandomierz. Two days later, Zhukov's First Byelorussian Front burst into action with an artillery barrage of enormous proportions, an infantry-break-in about ten miles deep, and then the almost-ritual release of Katukov and Bogdanov and their respective First and Second Guards Tank Armies in a drive for the Oder. To the north, Rokossovsky's tanks were driving through the defences which covered East Prussia.

Legend
- Front line Feb. 1 1945
- Russian attacks in Silesia Feb. Mar.
- Front line Feb. 24
- Russian attacks in Pomerania Feb. Mar.
- Front line Front line Mar. 31

0 ____ 80 Miles
0 ____ 120 Kilometres

BALTIC SEA

Hel
Peninsula
Bay of
Danzig

1st GDS.
TK. ARMY

Gdynia
Sopot
Danzig

II ARMY

Kolberg • **Köslin**

Belgard • Rummelsburg

Prechlau

Swinemünde

Stettiner
Haff

1st GDS.
TK. ARMY
Gross Radow

**ARMY GROUP
VISTULA
(Heinrici)**

III PZ. ARMY

III PZ. ARMY
(From Feb. 23)

Falkenburg

Graw

XI ARMY

Grudziadz

Neustrelitz

Stettin Gollnow Altdamn Stargard

Deutsch
Krone

Sepolno

**2nd BELORUSSIAN
FRONT** (Rokossovsky)

Prenzlau

Arnswalde

Schneidemuhl

Pyritz

**GERMAN
COUNTERATTACKS
FEB. 16/18**

Notec

Bydgoszcz

Vistula

Zehden Königsberg

5th SHOCK
ARMY

8th GDS.
ARMY

Inowroclaw

■ **Berlin** Kustrin

**1st BELORUSSIAN FRONT
(Zhukov)**

Poznan

POLAND

IX ARMY

Frankfurt

Fürstenberg

Warta

• Kolo

•Lübben

Guben

Cottbus• Forst

Bober

Grunberg

Oder

Glogau

Krotoszyn

Steinau

**1st UKRAINIAN
FRONT (Koniev)**

Neisse

*IV PZ.
ARMY*

Rotenburg

Bunzlau

Liegnitz

Breslau

Bautzen•

Dresden•

Görlitz

Lauban

4th TK.
ARMY

5th
GDS.
ARMY

21st ARMY

G

XVII ARMY

Strehlen

Oppeln

S

Grottkau

I

E

Neisse

LIV
CORPS

**ARMY GROUP
CENTRE
(Schörner)**

Elbe

S

Neustadt

Kosel

59th
ARMY

Prague ■

L

Ratibor

60th
ARMY

Katowice

A

Opava

**PART OF
I PZ. ARMY**

38th ARMY

N

D

C Z E C H O S L O V A K I A

G E R M A N Y

Strengthening the line: the Russians clear out Pomerania and Silesia

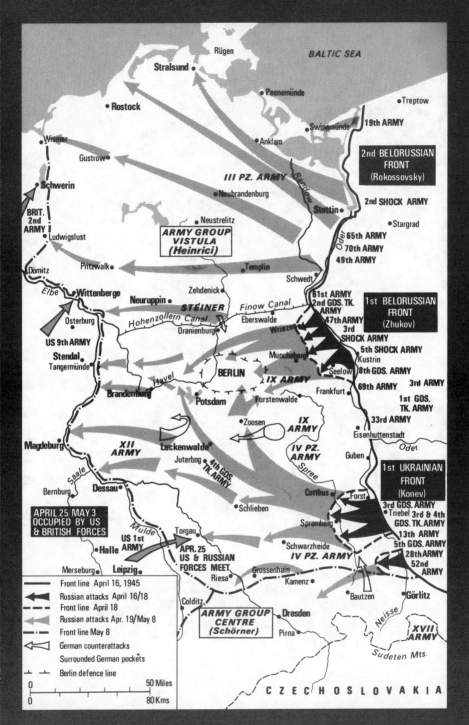

The last offensive: Berlin is surrounded and the Allies meet on the Elbe

Left: Russian troops, riding a T34/85 tank, are welcomed by the citizens of Prague.
Above: The Russians celebrate   the liberation of Ostrava, in May 1945, with a
review of the First Tank Brigade. *Below:* The T34s enter Minsk

Above left: T34s advance on Budapest under fire. *Left:* The Russian offensive January and February 1945: T34s advance in the snow. *Above:* A T34/85 carries infantrymen into the attack at the River Spree, April 1945

Immediately, another armoured race, not unlike that of the summer, began across the Polish plains. Zhukov entered the ruins of Warsaw on the 17th, and two days later Koniev's armour rolled across the Silesian border into the *Reich*. In Poland, the Russian tank formations were approaching the fantastic rate of advance of fifty miles a day. Before the end of January, they were moving on Brandenburg and Pomerania, and Zhukov's spearheads were no more than forty miles from Berlin. Koniev, too, hooking up towards the German capital from the south-east, seized the east bank of the Oder around Breslau. The capture of Berlin seemed only days away.

Now, however, there was a halt – not

for a few days, or even for a week or so, but until 16th April. The reasons for this pause have been much discussed in the West, and have been the subject of much argument, some of it surprisingly bitter, between Russian commanders. Chuikov, the hero of Stalingrad, who was commanding the Eighth Guards Army at Berlin, has asserted boldly that 'Berlin could have been taken in February, and this would, of course, have brought an earlier end to the war . . .' It has been said, too, that Stalin paused for political reasons, perhaps not wanting the war to end until he had made decisive gains in Hungary and Czechoslovakia.

Yet viewed from a strictly military standpoint, the reasons of *Stavka* for halting Zhukov and Koniev seem eminently sound. The Russian advance was primarily a tank advance – and just as in the previous summer, the Russian tanks were again overstretched. As the German line contracted around Berlin, so German troops became thicker to the mile,

The last hours in Berlin: Stalin tanks near the Reichstag

and the desperate quality of enemy resistance, even from *Volkssturm* units, was causing heavy losses which were not quickly replaced along shattered and congested lines of communication. There was a shortage of fuel and ammunition, both of which had to be hauled from dumps back on the Vistula.

Zhukov himself – perhaps sensing that Koniev intended at least that they should march side by side into the German capital – informed Stalin on 25th January that he intended to cross the Oder and, by implication, race to Berlin. Stalin's reaction was immediate. He pointed out that a great gap of almost one hundred miles was opening up between the right and left flanks of Zhukov and Rokossovsky respectively – and that Koniev would be in position to guarantee Zhukov's other flank while he was engaged

round Breslau. A glance at the map shows that this was an extremely cogent objection. Its relevance was borne out in the next few days.

Zhukov now discovered to his alarm that considerable German forces were gathered in Pomerania, creating such a severe threat to his right flank that he was forced to detach Katukov and Bogdanov and send their T-34s hurrying to the north. A day or two later, he was forced to transfer his First Tank Army to help Rokossovsky take Gdynia. For the moment, the clearing of the Baltic coast, in an attempt to neutralise the flank threat of the German forces still in eastern Pomerania, took precedence over operations farther south. Meanwhile the yawning gap between the First and Second Byelorussian Fronts was plugged only by cavalry. It was a fine opportunity for the Germans, had they had enough left of a unified command to take it, and it is also an interesting illustration of the fact that a rapid tank advance could storm the mind even of a general as hard-headed as Zhukov, leading him into the old, risky gambles of cavalry warfare through the ages.

However, probably the best reason of all for stopping was the tank state of Zhukov's tank armies. According to his own figures, these were down on 1st February to 740 tanks – an average of 40 to a brigade, with some brigades down to only 15. It is not surprising that, writing after the war, Zhukov seems to have come round to *Stavka*'s opinion. 'History shows,' he says, 'that risks should be taken, but not blindly . . .'

The final planning of the Berlin offensive was made on 1st April. Zhukov and Koniev met Stalin at his study in the Kremlin. Also present were the Chief of Staff, Antonov and the head of operations, Shtemenko. Stalin was now worried that a quick thrust by the Western Allies might actually give Berlin to the British and Americans before the Russians themselves could take the city. He set a deadline for the assault – April 16th. Berlin was finally to be mopped up by the end of the month. Koniev had already expressed his perturbation that the demarcation line between him and Zhukov meant that his armour would be forced too far south to strike at Berlin. Antonov, on his behalf, now pointed out to Stalin that a too-rigid adherence to the original plan might delay the final victory. Koniev himself has described what happened:

'. . . He began to pencil the line of demarcation, specified in the directives, on the map. It ran through Lubben, and on just south of Berlin. As he was tracing it, Stalin suddenly stopped at Lubben, which is roughly fifty miles south-east of Berlin, and made no further mark. Though he said nothing as he did so, we soldiers – myself no less than Marshal Zhukov – considered that his failure to trace the line further into the heart of Germany was significant . . . For me

at any rate, the stopping of the line at Lubben meant that if the breakthrough was rapid and operations swift and mobile on our right flank, a situation could well develop in which it would be of advantage for us to attack Berlin from the south . . .'

From this point on, there is no doubt as to the spirit in which Koniev viewed his task. He immediately stationed on his right flank Rybalko's Third and Lelyushenko's Fourth Guards Tank Armies. Zhukov, also disposing of two Guards Tank Armies, put Bogdanov in the north of his sector and Katukov in the south each supported by two or three infantry armies.

In many ways, Zhukov faced a tougher problem than Koniev. His armour was to strike for the heart of the city, and it was a bigger, more complex, more difficult city than tanks had ever fought inside in the history of war. Obviously such a vast network of roads, sewers, tunnels and railways, spreading for 350 square miles, presented a serious problem for armour, both from enfilade fire in the criss-cross of streets and avenues, and from the roofs and windows of buildings.

Zhukov decided to begin his assault on the German line of defence running through the outlying villages two hours before dawn, and to illuminate the line of advance for the tanks with searchlights. At five on the morning of the 16th, his Front's artillery crashed its preliminary barrage down on the German positions, supported by low-flying aircraft and fighter-bombers. Then, under the glare of 140 searchlights, the tanks went in. In fact, the searchlights were regarded as a mixed blessing by some Russian commanders, who said later that they made it difficult to get an overall picture of the battle. Zhukov's progress, especially when he came up against the defences of the Seelow heights, was slower than had been hoped. The Front's northern wing had pushed forward no more than

two to five miles, while in the south Katukov's First Guards Tank Army had done better, driving into the German defences up to a depth of eight miles.

Stalin was already worried by Zhukov's slow progress, and he cast his eyes further south. Down there, Koniev had had more success, crashing over the Neisse river under a heavy smokescreen on the 16th, and putting through his armour in the afternoon. The tanks tore a gap more than fifteen miles wide, and within twenty-four hours had advanced more than eleven miles. The threat which Koniev now posed to the German rear was too good to waste, however galling it might be to Zhukov. During the 17th, *Stavka* ordered a willing Koniev to turn north and drive on Berlin.

On the 18th and 19th, Zhukov made better progress, though the German defence was so desperate that he could find no opportunity to release his two tank armies. Both Katukov and Bogdanov remained closely linked with their infantry. Slowly the attack ground on, and by the 25th Lelyushenko's Fourth Guards Tank Army of Koniev's command had joined hands with Bogdanov's Second Guards Tank Army of Zhukov's command, so that Berlin was now surrounded. Rumbling into the city, often driving through office blocks and shops in an effort to take ground without exposing themselves in the dangerous streets, the Russian tanks neared the heart of Berlin. By the 27th, they had reached the Potsdamer Platz, only a few hundred yards from the doomed Führer's headquarters. Hitler's bunker now shook to the shells of Russian armour. In the hours before he shot himself on 30th April 1944, those who ventured up to the desolate garden of the Chancellery above the bunker could hear little from the outside world, except the thud of gunfire and the steady rumble of the tracks of the T-34s.

The symbol

In many ways, the T-34 symbolised the whole spirit and nature of the Russian struggle from 1941 to 1945, and embodied the basic reasons for the final victory. It was, perhaps, a crude machine in Western eyes, dispensing with much in the way of comfort and sophistication that were considered desirable, even essential, in the tanks of Britain, Germany, and the United States. Paradoxically, it probably won more trust from its crews than any comparable weapon in any army: the Sherman was a fine tank, but by the time it appeared it was already being overtaken by new German designs: the Panther was arguably the best tank of the war, but it was used by crews who, by that time, were fighting a losing war.

The great strength of the T-34 was its concentration on essentials – gun, armour, mobility. No tank, in 1940, had ever embodied these qualities so successfully, or balanced them so well. To the Russians, the lack of crew comfort, and the crudeness of some of the ancillary equipment, were of less importance than they might have seemed farther west. The Russian crews who manned the T-34/76 and the T-34/85 were not – indeed, could not have been – precisely the same kind of young men who crewed the Mark III, the Sherman or the Crusader. The nature of pre-war Russia meant that they had virtually no chance of having driven, let alone owned, a private motor car. The automobile and the internal combustion engine were not a hobby to them, as they were to many in Britain and Germany and the United States. They were trained from the raw: peasants were taken from villages and taught how to drive, gun and command the T-34 in battle. Under such circumstances, men accept the equipment that they are given, and do not feel the lack of what they have never had.

Cavalry, old and new styles: American built Shermans, Russian mounted troops

Above all, what the T-34 gave to the Russian soldier, high and low, was confidence – a confidence on which the later brilliant successes of the Russian tank army could later be securely built. It is interesting to reflect what might have happened if the excellence of Mikhail Koshkin's design had not been developed in time. if the T-34 had still been on the drawing board when the Germans struck in 1941. There would have been no fine general purpose chassis on which to build, no basis for simplified production as the factories were torn up in the industrial retreat to the Urals – for the chassis of the KV-I, the other available Russian tank, was much more limited in use than that of the T-34. There would have been no technological superiority for Russian armour to help balance the inferiorities in training and crews with which it began the campaign. The whole flood of T-34 tanks and SU vehicles which Zhukov and Koniev used so well in mass might have been very much smaller in volume if its manufacture had had to start even a year later. The consequences in deciding the issue of the campaign could hardly be over-estimated. Just like the designers of the British eight-gun fighters, Koshkin

Above: A British Crusader tank cruiser
Right: KV1A tank in Moscow

and his team made a decisive contribution to the history of the world.

However, even more impressive than the development of the weapon was the astonishing production of the crews who were to use it. Yet this phenomenon, one of the most astounding in the history of war, has been largely overshadowed by the praise given to the forces on the other side – the German panzer divisions. The glamour and rattle of the panzer divisions, criss-crossing Europe on their missions of conquest and destruction, have seized the hearts and minds of military analysts all over the world – an enthusiasm compounded by copious memoirs from the German Panzer leaders in which the feeling of having created and belonged to a military elite is given full play. That the panzer divisions brought success but not victory is a truth which, even now, has not been fully grasped.

For, in the end, it was the Russians who made the most enduring contribution to the theory and practice of armoured war. This theory bound the foot soldier to the tank much more closely than had been fashion-

able in the West since 1918; it sought a much more thorough destruction of the enemy front – usually by artillery, infantry and heavy tanks – before mobile forces were released; it kept a much tighter hand on mobile armour, even when released, than would have been acceptable to men like Rommel and Guderian. It did not produce whistles of astonishment at the skill and daring of commanders and crews. It produced victory.

Its basis was mass. In this context, mass use of tanks meant mass training of crews, and it is in this field that one of the greatest Russian achievements lay. To have taken tens of thousands of factory workers, clerks and peasants, and made them in a necessarily short space of time into commanders, drivers, loaders, and gunners for the T-34, was by itself a considerable feat – requiring training facilities and instructors and schools on an enormous scale, all created under the crisis of battle. Even more impressive, perhaps, was the creation of the great infrastructure necessary for armoured battle: the supply services, tank workshops, breakdown teams, traffic control units, communications networks, and the rest. A tank army cannot advance 450 miles in five weeks, as the Russians did in the summer of 1944, without staff and technical organisation of the highest class. More even than this, it needs morale, discipline, enthusiasm, and determination. Whoever, in the Russian tank schools, was turning out the crews who manned Zhukov's, Koniev's and Rotmistrov's tanks was succeeding in training them up to a level at which they were capable of meeting in battle the somewhat self-conscious élite of Nazi Germany. The crews matched the weapon, and in the case of the T-34, at any rate, that was a high standard to set.

As for the weapon itself, it has lingered on. There are few tanks produced in the last twenty years that do not owe something to the thinking of Mikhail Koshkin in 1939. The T-34 is still good enough to go into battle, and did so as recently as the Arab-Israel war of 1967. We might, however, leave the last word to a German panzer commander, Field-Marshal Ewald von Kleist, who suffered more than most from the attentions of the T-34. It was he, it will be remembered, who said simply that it was 'the finest tank in the world . . .'

Bibliography

Barbarossa by Alan Clark (Hutchinson, London. New American Library, New York)

Russia at War by Alexander Werth (Barrie & Rockliffe, London. Avon Books, New York)

Panzer Leader by Heinz Guderian (Michael Joseph, London. Ballantine, New York)

Marshal Zhukov's Greatest Battles by George K Zhukov (Macdonald, London. Harper and Row, New York)

The Soviet High Command by John Erickson (Macmillan, London. St Martin, New York)

Juggernaut by Malcom Mackintosh (Secker & Warburg, London. Macmillan, New York)

Panzer Battles by F W von Mellenthin (Cassell, London. University of Oklahoma Press, Norman, Oklahoma)

Hitler's War on Russia by Paul Carell (Harrap, London)

The Beginning of the Road by Marshal Vassily Chuikov (Macgibbon & Kee, London)

Armour by Richard Ogorkiewicz (Stevens, London)

Design and Development of Fighting Vehicles by Richard Ogorkiewicz (Macdonald, London. Doubleday, New York)

Lost Victories by Eric von Manstein (Methuen, London)

German Tanks of World War II by F von Senger and Etterlin (Arms and Armour Press, London. Stackpole, Harrisburg, Pa.)

Memoirs, by Albert Kesselring. (William Kimber)

Also see series of five articles in Airfix magazine, July-November 1968, by John Milsom.